My
Father's
Footprints

My Father's Footprints

A MEMOIR

Colin McEnroe

WARNER BOOKS

An AOL Time Warner Company

"Telemachus' Detachment from *Meadowlands* by Louise Glück. Copyright ©
1996 by Louise Glück. Reprinted by permission of HarperCollins Publishers
Inc.

Material from "Faerieland" by Colin McEnroe in *Northeast Magazine,* June
21, 1992. Copyright *The Hartford Courant*. Reprinted with permission.

"Let's Wait" by Pablo Neruda, copyright 1992. Reprinted by permission of
Grove Atlantic.

"I Wouldn't Bet One Penny," published by Warner Chappell, copyright 1961 by
Johnny Burke; copyright renewed 1989 by Mary Kramer, Rory Burke, Timolin
Burke Goldfarb, and Reagan Drew. Reprinted by permission.

Warner Books, Inc., 1271 Avenue of the Americas, New York, NY 10020
Visit our Web site at www.twbookmark.com.

An AOL Time Warner Company

The Library of Congress Cataloging-in-Publication Data
McEnroe, Colin.
    My father's footprints : a memoir / Colin McEnroe.
        p. cm.
    ISBN 0-446-52933-8
        1. McEnroe, Colin—Family. 2. Humorists, American—20th century—
Biography. 3. Fathers—Death—Psychological aspects. 4. Parent and adult
child—United States. 5. Baby boom generation—United States. 6. Fathers
and sons—United States. I. Title.

PS3563.C3615 M9 2003
818'.5402—dc21
[B]   2002191018

Printed in the United States of America

First Printing: July 2003
10 9 8 7 6 5 4 3 2 1

Text design by Meryl Sussman Levavi / Digitext

Acknowledgments

My friend, colleague, and in-law Steve Metcalf used to play the organ in a gospel church, and when it came time for members to stand and give personal testimony, a certain woman would rise and mention—among the many blessings afforded her by heaven—"My friends all know me."

The meaning of this is obscure and, in another way, obvious. It's sort of the ultimate acknowledgment. If my friends all know me, what else do I need to say?

(My secret fear is that I will acknowledge people who were barely aware of this project and whose absentminded "hmmmph"s and "mmmmmmm"s I over-embraced as encouragement. And now they see their names here and think: I was one of his pillars? He must be desperate.)

This project took shape mainly with the help of my old colleagues at the *Hartford Courant*, led by Kyrie O'Connor and

Acknowledgments

Lary Bloom, and with the support of *Men's Health* magazine, where Peter Moore and his crew took a chance on an essay that became chapter one of this book. The Books for a Better Life people honored that essay and drew the attention of Warner Books. Many thanks to the endlessly patient Karen Melnyk and her successor, Katharine Rapkin.

Esther Newberg is my agent. So watch out.

I thank also my colleagues at WTIC for putting up with my absences and states of distraction. I had friends who helped in ways immeasurable and measurable. These include Peter and Sally Shapiro, Bill Curry, Denise Merrill, Jessie Stratton, Frank Rich, and Bill Heald. Susan Campbell did not hit me (even) once during the writing of this book.

Epic gratitude to Luanne Rice, all-knowing, all-seeing, all-giving, and Anne Batterson, who rescued me and my book from all kinds of mistakes.

Thanks to the good people of Mountnugent, especially those mentioned in chapter five, and to Susan McKeown, for the inspiring music of "Lowlands."

Some of the names in this book were changed, but I'm not saying which ones.

Thanks to all of you who believed in my father's work, during his life and afterward. Thanks to all the family members who supported me, especially my wife, Thona, and son, Joey. For rights to use Joey's image in "My Father's Footprints—The Video Game," you need to negotiate directly with his people.

And thanks most of all to my mother, who could have vetoed the whole idea and didn't.

Contents

Preface   1

1. Seal Barks and Whale Songs   3

2. Why Nobody Understands Turbulence   39

3. Bliss   85

4. MOST HaPPy FIMLY   123

5. Straight Outta Roscommon or
   Why History Can Be So Hortful   144

6. In Which the Court Adjourns   184

Epilogue   195

My
Father's
Footprints

When I was a child looking
at my parents' lives, you know
what I thought? I thought
heartbreaking. Now I think
heartbreaking, but also
insane. Also
very funny.

"TELEMACHUS' DETACHMENT"
BY LOUISE GLÜCK

Preface

On the most beautiful evening of the spring of 2002, we ride our bikes, Joey and I, and somehow wind up at the grave.

Joey is twelve now, four years older, very different, and yet exactly the same as the boy you will meet in this book. Embedded in the earth is a small granite slab into which his grandfather's name has been cut. He doesn't like to see me step onto it.

"Don't stand on it!"

"Why not? Bob's not here. He's not underneath this stone."

Joey climbs up on a reddish-brown boulder next to the grave. My mother and I picked the site partly because of the boulder.

"Where is he?"

"Maybe in the air around us."

In the pine trees behind the boulder, someone has hung chimes, and they ding softly in the breeze.

"Is that it? Is he in the air around us? Or is it: When you die, you die?" Joey demands.

"Some people think that."

"Is that what you think?"

"I think it's possible that we become something greater."

"What does that mean?"

"Well," I fumble, "when we're in these bodies . . . we suffer from sorrow, need, guilt, hunger, pain, fear . . ."

"Dad, that's *your* life," he interrupts, and I laugh. He laughs, too.

"What I was going to say," I resume at last, "is that maybe when we die, we become something more pure and more joined-together with everything else. Maybe we move beyond those limitations of sorrow and pain."

"Maybe we're born into another body," Joey says. "Maybe it's like one of my video games. You have to get to Level Ten before you get out."

We fall silent, and only the chimes speak.

"This is movie-like, with the ringing," he says at last. He gestures in a way that takes in the whole scene and, I think, the conversation. "It's like a movie."

I look at him, and love, dark and fiery, rips through me. He has thickened with preadolescent chunkiness. Wriggling into his Latino identity, he has been hanging with the Puerto Rican kids at school, cribbing their fashions. He wears chains and robin's egg–blue Carolina football shirts and bulky dark denim shorts that droop to the knee. He is a long way from the little boy who darted like a beach bird across the early days of this story. I will love him with every drop of my lifeblood no matter who he is.

We get our bikes and ride home swiftly. I want to write it all down before it changes in my head. And I do, scribbling it verbatim onto a series of five Post-Its, the first pieces of paper I find.

But first there's the bike ride out of the cemetery with the sun low in the west, like a hole in the sky-side, letting the gold stream in, across the trees, heavy with spring flowers, across the stern white slabs of the dead.

Emerson said heaven walks among us, so maybe my father is here, gleaming in all that slanting golden afternoon light.

One

Seal Barks and Whale Songs

Sarah Whitman Hooker Pies
recommended with this chapter
- ◆ Mother Teresa's Mouse Pie for
  religious cats, bats, and owls
- ◆ Westinghouse Six-Stroke Air Pie
  with jelly beans and old subway tokens
- ◆ The Green Bastard

છજ

The last time my father died was in 1998. It differed from his other deaths in that, this time, we buried him. The McEnroes were, until recently, the sort of Irish-American family that favored florid Irish wakes. I remember my parents returning from one of the last good ones, around 1970. They were pretty well lit, and my mother explained that one of the McEnroes, a man in the liquor business as it happened, parked a station wagon loaded with potables in the funeral home parking lot. The mourners would filter out there, have a nip, and return to the parlor, their enthusiasm for the wake and their nostalgia for the dead vastly refreshed.

Their bodies heavy with weeping and their minds sodden with drink, they eventually managed to lock the keys inside the station wagon. Very quickly, it came to pass that getting the station wagon unlocked was the thing of paramount importance, so that virtually everyone who had been inside the funeral home was now out in the parking lot giving advice and jiggling coat hangers. The poor corpse was left alone with one or two sniffling women.

My father was faintly amused, but it was, he said, a puny affair compared to the wakes of distant summers.

"Then," he said, "the women would keen, making such an awful high-pitched racket you thought you were going to lose your mind. And when the men were drunk enough, they'd haul the body out of the casket and prop it up in a chair, put a drink in one hand and a cigarette in the other."

He paused and smiled, letting his hazel eyes wander up in the air to where the memories floated like dust motes.

"The whole idea," he said, a little dreamily, "was to make sure the son of a bitch was really dead."

The last time my father died, the son of a bitch really was.

❧

It starts in 1996.

I'm with my father, on a spring afternoon in West Hartford, Connecticut, where we all live, watching my son, who has just learned to ride his bike.

Where we live, the forested reservoir lands are also parks. Paved roads, dedicated to hikers, joggers, and bikers, curl and course through the gorgeous woods.

I see Joey launching himself onto those roads, sailing away in looping arcs, out to where my father cannot follow.

Joey is adopted. He is Mexican, and his skin is the beautiful color of coffee ice cream. In the summer, it deepens into a coppery chocolate. His eyes are wide and brown and startling.

My father's hair is white as summer clouds, and his skin is ruddy from rosacea and Irishness. His body is thickset. In appearance, he has been compared, variously, to Chet Huntley and Spencer Tracy, although neither was ever as handsome, or as fey, as my father in his prime. His face is craggy, rugged. Merriment and sadness play across it in constant shifting patterns, the way those summer clouds, moving in the wind, might push light and shadow across the land.

I help my father from a car to a chair. He is stiff with spinal stenosis, shaky from late-onset diabetes, clutched by congestive heart failure.

There is something else I cannot see and do not know. Cirrhosis from secret late-night drinking sessions is scourging his liver.

In two years, he will be gone, and I will join the Dead Fathers Society.

At the moment, I feel only the twitching of life's giant clockworks. I feel as though the very mechanism of life requires my father to slow down as my son accelerates.

It feels satisfactory and right.

Maybe it is, too, but not in the nice, neat way I'm imagining.

ॐ

Now it is 1997.

Mockernut. Pignut. Shagbark. Tulip Poplar. Red Oak.

There are little signs on some of the trees as you roll through the roads of the reservoir. A year has passed. Today Joey is on foot, and Bob is in a wheelchair. He has grown sicker, and I take him on outings.

Today I am trying to wheel him along the 3.6-mile course of the reservoir, which takes in some pretty steep hills. Descending them, I lean backward at sharp angles, like a man walking wild boars on a leash. Occasionally I pop a hand loose from one of the grips to either throw or catch a squishy little football Joey and I are playing with as we walk.

I have come to think of these excursions as the Sandwich Generation Triathlon. Walk, Push, Throw.

My father has now been diagnosed. He is terminal. We don't talk about that. We don't talk about anything unpleasant, but my father can see that I have, for months, devoted my free time to him. I have driven him to medical appointments and taken him on these walks and slogged through shopping trips.

One day I take him to an art museum and dilate upon the meanings of the paintings. In front of a Winslow Homer, a pretty woman smiles at us, and I think she likes me for taking such good care of my dad.

A minute later I realize she was gently amused, because my pedantic lecture has sent the patient into a deep sleep.

Still, when he gets home he tells my mother, "It was like a different world."

My dad is mainly housebound.

One day I wheel him around the neighborhood in the sleepy afternoon sun, and I sing Johnny Mercer songs to him. "Skylark," "On the Atchison, Topeka and the Santa Fe," "That Old Black Magic," "Ac-cent-tchu-ate the Positive." He likes that a lot. I'll never forget that day, singing to my father.

Occasionally, as we wangle the wheelchair through a tricky doorway, he will mumble, "Who would have thought . . . that you would turn out to be so useful."

❧

If you have a spouse, a child, a dog or two, a sick father, a worried and very tired mother, one way to get through a long, hard Sunday is to make a list of tasks. You start it at 6:30 A.M. and keep crossing items off, glancing down to the bottom of the list where there awaits, you presume, a paradise. You will park your tired self on a sofa and maybe watch *The X-Files,* because at least the guy who is part-fluke and who lives in the sewers will have a life slightly worse than your own.

Even under the iron rule of a list, Joey and I sneak in a bit of fun, tossing a football in a deserted parking lot and walking at dusk, with the dogs, into spooky, empty, snow-dusted woods. Just as the air around us fades from gray to black we stand in the pie-powdery snow on the banks of a chilling stream. And it's so heartbreakingly weird and beautiful you wonder why people don't come here by the hundreds.

And then back to work.

Last thing on the list: Bake cookies. I forget why. For school?

I'm halfway into the baking when my mother calls.

It's 8:45 P.M.

My butt is feeling a sort of magnetic pull toward the promised land of the sofa.

"Can you come over? Something is wrong with Dad."

Ohhhhhhhhh. For a brief moment, I am unsure which is the greater tragedy—my father's ill health or the fact that I'm not going to sit down and watch television.

I drive over, and, indeed, he is failing in some ineffable way, dead on his feet, muddled in his head. I bring him into the bedroom and try to get him settled into bed, but his body flops and sprawls, starting to slide toward the floor.

I haul him up again.

"Let me try to get your head in the right place," I grunt.

"I've always wanted my head in the right place," he murmurs slurrily.

He's about ten synapse-firings this side of a coma, and he's still funny.

The next day I discover the interrupted cookies. They have congealed into a rubbery texture. Eating one would be like a hyena eating Gumby.

&

Things are worse, much worse.

I sit down with my mother and my father's doctor.

"We should get hospice involved," I say.

There's an awkward silence. The doctor has to authorize this. He has to say that the patient is terminally ill. He has to say that the patient will not live more than six months. You can get extensions. They don't send a guy in a hood with a scythe if you miss the deadlines. All the same . . .

"I'm reluctant to take that step," he says. "When you say the word 'Hospice' to a patient, it's almost like a death sentence."

I look at him.

"Well," I say, "he is dying, isn't he?"

The doctor kind of shrugs.

He is an old-school guy, operates out of a big white house on a main avenue. He was taught that you fix people until you can't fix them anymore. Then you let Nature take over and hope it's quick. This idea of giving Death an extended booking, two shows a night with a pit orchestra, is hard for him to grasp.

My father, by all rights, should be dead by now, but my mother refuses to let this happen. When Dad begins to sag into a coma, she ignores the doctor's advice and summons an ambulance to take my father to a hospital, where he is transfused and revived, just as Death was set to swoop in and claim him.

My mother is a small, unassuming woman with downcast eyes. In a room full of people you might miss her. I think it's possible that Death underestimated her. She wears her hair permed up and back in a kind of sixties bouffant, dyeing it this shade and that, making all the stops on a subway line from blonde to auburn. My wife's hair, by contrast, turned a silvery white in her forties, and she let it stay that way. Her face is utterly unlined, making her white hair seem as anomalous as my mother's ash blonde hair hovering over an older face. My mother's voice has stayed musical and girlish, in defiance of all the cigarettes she smoked, a pleasant echo of the beauty she once was.

The doctor now believes he is caught in an unpredictable crossfire between Death and this very tiny woman. He has absolutely no idea what to do, and his plan is to meet with us as rarely as possible, return few phone calls, and check the obit page to see if this mess has, by any chance, resolved itself.

❧

It takes a few weeks of my jiggling the handle, and then my father is a hospice patient.

This means we are all resigned to keeping him comfortable, easing his pain, soothing his soul, letting him die.

Except my mother.

"I made a commitment," she says, repeatedly. No one can remember hearing her make this commitment, but apparently it has the force of something you might say while pulling Excalibur out of a rock. The commitment includes keeping my father at home and administering medicines and meals with a precision and doggedness no hospital could achieve. My mother is *Star Trek*'s Borg Collective, a flying cube of quasi-mechanical imperialism. My father will take his medicine at the exact time prescribed. He will eat balanced meals, three times a day. Assimilate or be destroyed. Resistance is futile. My father lives an extra nine months or so because he is almost too busy to die.

Paid caregivers from the outside are held to rigorous standards of conduct.

"Where's the hospice aide?" I ask one day, darting into the apartment in between work and home.

"I fired hospice," my mother says.

"Very funny."

"I did."

"Nobody fires hospice. That's like . . . I mean . . . um . . . they're the last word in . . . last words." I concede that this is not exactly Martin Luther King Jr.'s "I Have a Dream" speech. I'm kind of babbling while my mind bids farewell to all those brisk, competent hospice workers who were—I had thought—going to get me through those moments when I'm weak and exhausted and afraid, like right now, for instance.

"Hospice are the people who take care of you when you have nobody else," I try again. "Everybody likes hospice." (Possible title for final *Raymond* episode?)

It's no use. My mother is scared. Her response to fearfulness and isolation has always been to set up an even more fearful and isolating situation. The hospice people are *not helping enough*. So they must go.

We find a different hospice agency and reenlist.

"You have to promise not to fire them, even if the aides show up late," I beg.

"I'm not promising anything."

My mother does most of the work and grows so tired that we arrange a five-day respite for her. My father will go to a beautiful nursing home in the woods.

Early one morning, I drive my father out to the McLean Home for this short stay. I step through the sliding doors and behold the sunlit atrium, the California fireplace, the greenhouse, the smiling and friendly staff, the soft jazz playing in the lobby. It is impossibly peaceful and cheerful.

"You don't happen to have a second bed available, do you?" I inquire weakly.

The soft jazz turns out to be a man playing, perhaps a little dementedly, the Natalie Cole version of "Avalon" over and over, but in all other respects, McLean appears to be paradise on earth for the middle-aged, the weary, the sandwiched. I don't want to leave.

❧

Conversation between me and my son, who is eight.
"Does anybody live to be one hundred twenty?"
"Not very often."
"How old will I be when I die?"
"Old, I hope."
"Will you live to be one hundred? How old will I be when you're one hundred?"
"Sixty-five. We can be old men together."
I get a lot of this these days. It's evening, and Joey and I are driving back from McLean. He's a trouper about visiting my father, but spending a lot of time around the very old, around the near-to-death, has stirred up questions in him.
"Do really old people want to die?"
"Sometimes. Sometimes people who are ninety or one hundred say they feel they've lived enough; they're tired in some way we can't even begin to understand."
We come up over a rise in Simsbury, and Hartford surprises us, twinkling in the distance. Life is long, life is short. We're just guests here, checking off tasks, getting through our lists. The car surges through the night. There's a lot to talk about.

When the five days are over, I drive out to bring my dad home to my mother. I have slipped into some horrific high-functioning mode, where my voice booms out cheery good advice to him and my manner is that of a bustling and businesslike male nurse.

This is precisely what my father does not need. He needs some humanity from me. He needs to visit with me in the kind, intensely personal way that a father may visit with a son. I do not give him that. I give him an officious, hearty, no-nonsense parody of myself

"I thought we might eat lunch together," he mumbles weakly.

"No time for me to eat!" I boom, with a big false smile. "I've got to get you all packed up, load up the car, get everything squared away with the people here while you eat."

I have become a Sim. "The Sims" is a computer game in which you build digital people and orchestrate their lives. They marry, have babies, get sick, lose jobs. They seem to set themselves on fire by accident a lot. You assign personal traits to each one, but the palette of emotional colors is pretty limited.

I read that in 2001, the people who play "The Sims" noticed an odd phenomenon. Their fake people would begin to cough and then die, in uncommonly large numbers. The players began discussing this on Internet message boards and discovered a common denominator. The game company's Web site allowed players to add new furnishings, accessories, and other items not originally included on the disc. The people whose Sims contracted this unexplained Simtheria had all downloaded an extra pet, a guinea pig, and had been delinquent about making the Sims clean its cage.

The company admitted that, yes, the guinea pigs were programmed to give the people, in some circumstances, a fatal disease. Behind that lay a deeper, more troubling truth. The "things" in the Sims world were all impregnated with programming that elicited certain responses. The Sims appeared to have rich identities, but that was an illusion. They were pretty empty, but their environments were just loaded with invisible personality fragments that could be activated if touched.

This is how I feel, during these trying times. Not like a person with real emotional depth but like the framework for a person. Some kid's hand on a mouse is moving me through my days, and when I brush up against a wheelchair or a wristwatch, I may smile or cry, but it's just the thing I touched doing a data dump into my hollow self.

Even so, there is no excuse for my fake joviality here in the elysian nursing home. But have you ever had that feeling? That if you gave one inch to your true emotions, you'd be in a free fall? Easier to be a Sim.

The next day, I bring my faithful and true twelve-year-old mongrel dog, Roy, to the vet for more tests. He appears to have liver problems, as does my father, which makes one wonder if I have somehow offended the Liver God.

By bedtime, I am so tired that I have my father and Roy's problems hopelessly conflated in my head. I know one of them is under strict orders not to eat any more dead animals in the woods.

Conversation between me and my son, about our aging but preternaturally young-looking dog.

"How old is Roy?"

"Twelve."

"How old would that be for a person?"

"I'm not sure. Do you multiply by seven? If so, he's . . . eighty-four."

"How can he be?"

"Good care, good food, lots of love. And I think he has good genes."

"What are genes?"

"The parts of your body that say a lot about your health and how you're going to be, in general."

"Do I have good genes?"

"I think you do."

"Do you have good genes?"

"Um. Probably only so-so."

"Who has the best genes?"

"I don't know." (I refuse to say Michael Jordan.)

(Said with amusement.) "Maybe God. He's been alive so long."

Later. Son, Mexican-American, regarding his brown-haired, brown-eyed guinea pig: "If I were a guinea pig, I would look just like Edward."

And now I recollect a conversation from a day in 1996, before the terrible sickness set down its giant scaly foot on us. My wife is telling my father that Roy is slowing down.

"That's what big dogs do. They slow down. They sleep more. They get quieter. It almost helps prepare you for the fact that they're going to die."

My father smiles fiendishly and inclines his head toward my mother.

"Could you please tell this to Barbara? It's exactly what I've been trying to do for years, and she won't let me."

❧

My father is slipping away, so that he can only answer the most basic questions. Are you hungry? Do you want to go to bed?

It's 2:00 A.M. when the phone rings.

I rush to my parents' apartment because my father is having a bad spell.

I get him settled in bed, get him calmed down, all very *Marvin's Room.* He looks at my mother and says, from his delirium, "How did Colin know how to make the spooks go away?"

"The spooks? What spooks? There are no spooks."

Have you ever noticed that dementia makes a person rather attractive to talk to? You can't stop yourself. It's kind of obsessively fun to argue them out of their delusions because, for once, you know you're right. There *are* no mauve bats flying barrel rolls in the room.

❀   ❀   ❀

Sometimes, on lovely days, I offer the park or the woods, and he makes me take him to depressing discount stores. He wants to buy a watch. He has dozens. He wants some writing equipment, but the work he is determined to write—some last gasp having to do with Dante—never comes to anything more than a few words scribbled here and there as his mind melts into a puddle.

"I'll pick those up for you," I say. "While you have me, why don't I take you someplace pretty, so you can get some sun and fresh air?"

He looks dejected.

"That's not fair," he says.

Exasperated, I load him and the wheelchair into my car and head off for Service Merchandise. He looks and looks at watches. He buys a certain one and takes it home. But it is the same as all the others. It shows time running out.

Two years after his death, I tear a quadriceps tendon playing soccer and Life finally teaches me what I refused to learn back then. My friends are willing to fetch me anything, take me anywhere; but one day, a couple of weeks after surgery, I sneak out, stagger to the corner in my full-leg brace before the neighbors see me and offer to help, and I catch the bus, go to a coffee shop, and buy myself lunch, just for the existential thrill of asserting myself in the consumer economy. I take out my wallet, pay the bill, get the change. This is very fulfilling, in a way I had not expected, as if it restored substance to the phantasm I was becoming.

In a capitalist age, I spend, therefore I am.

That's what my father craves. The ritual of the transaction.

By the time I understand this, he is long gone, and I remember, with rue, how edgy I was on those sunny days when I thought I knew what he needed better than he did.

❧

"Is he in pain?" the aide wants to know.

"No," I tell her distractedly. "It's something else."

We are standing in my father's bedroom. He sleeps more and more, and from his sleep he issues peculiar sounds. Short wordless vocal bursts in a single tone, easily mistaken for a groan, but closer—in their sporadic pattern and duration—to the gentle undersea songs of whales. What do whales say? "I'm here." "You're there." "You're there." "I'm here." Perhaps that's what my father does, from the half-sleep of life's end: announces himself to the world, trumpets out a hopeful sound, and listens for what bounces back. He gives a hoot.

When he gathers his wits, he often wants to talk—heretically—about God. In a public park, as I push him in his wheelchair, he suddenly stirs, rears up, and pretty much bellows, "What I don't understand is, if God wanted a son, why didn't he just make one? Why did that poor girl have to get *knocked up?*"

Today is the Super Bowl. I have rooted for the Green Bay Packers since I was about fourteen, which means I have endured twenty-five years of really awful teams until quite recently. I never had the chance to see them get near a Super Bowl until last year, when I was assigned a Sunday night radio show, so I missed the whole thing.

Care for the dying is as amenable to crass bargaining as any other human activity.

"I want to watch the Super Bowl tonight," I tell my mother. "I want to put in my hours this morning and this afternoon. By nightfall, I want to be replaced by paid health aides, hospice volunteers, or those guards in *The Wizard of Oz* who march wearing busbies and appear to be singing 'Oreo.' I am determined to watch the Super Bowl in an undisturbed setting where I can concentrate, yell, whoop, weep. Where I can be in the presence of similarly dedicated NFL fans and not people who are checking their watches and demanding to know why anybody cares about all this organized savagery."

Even as I speak these words, I am dimly aware that I am tempting the gods to gainsay me. I work with hospice to line up extra coverage and try to batten down every hatch that might fly open during the game.

And what happens? My father suddenly takes a turn for the worse, so much so that he cannot be left alone with my mother anymore. All of the coverage vanishes into the Mists of Healthcare.

Joey and I find ourselves waiting for kick-off in my parents' apartment, very possibly the worst place I can be, because (a) I may have to attend to my dad or take him to the bathroom at any moment; and (b) My mother disapproves of football and, during my childhood, would not allow us to watch it in the house because it led to excited yelling, which she also did not allow.

So Joey and I are watching, hunching down, and trying to be very quiet and dignified, although I am wearing a foam rubber Cheesehead.

From a spot somewhere behind us I hear my mother say, flatly, emphatically, to no one, "I hate Super Bowl."

Jeez.

᠈᠖

He always claimed to be an atheist, but he was way too engaged for that. He secretly wanted to be a heretic.

But it's time-consuming. And you have to go to meetings and listen to doctrine. I think my father wanted to be a heretic, not in some church, but right in God's face. I think he wanted to hang around God's office and argue with God about important stuff and get on God's nerves.

Sean Kennelly, a former Catholic priest, late of Ireland, one parish over from Donnybrook, shows up at my parents' apartment.

He has been phoning. He's a hospice pastoral counselor. He had to give up the priest thing so he could get married. He is a holy man but also full of the devil, in a nice way. My mother won't let him anywhere near Dad, but I can't make out whom she's protecting: Kennelly from my father's blasphemies or my father from any sense that this is last rites. Now Sean has decided to beard the lion in its den.

"Mrs. McEnroe, will you not let me up?" he says on the intercom.

"No, I'm afraid now is not a good time."

"That's what you always say. I'll only stay just a minute and say hello."

Such is Sean's charm that it works even on a squawk box. He gets in somehow. He and my father have a few talks, which they both seem to enjoy.

"I've seen the type before. 'I'm an atheist, praise be to God,'" Sean confides to me in his brogue.

❧

My father's moments of clarity come less often.

I bring over a videotape to watch with him. *Primal Fear* with Richard Gere. We watch three minutes; he nods off. I stop the tape. He wakes up. We watch ten minutes. He dozes. I stop the tape. He perks. We watch. Snooze. Stop. Wake. Watch. Now he is deeply, deeply asleep. I stop the tape and grab something to read. It seems wrong to watch without him.

Suddenly he stirs, shakes his head.

"What happened to Bang Bang Fuck You?" he demands.

"What?" I must be hearing things.

"Bang Bang Fuck You."

I stare at him.

"The movie!" he says, exasperated.

I start it up again, but now I can't stop giggling. Now I'm laughing so hard my eyes are watering.

I'm picturing the Oscars. "Accepting the Best Picture award for *Bang Bang Fuck You* is its producer, Leonard T. Salink."

Or the video store. "Do you have *Bang Bang Fuck You?*"

"All our copies of *Bang Bang Fuck You* are out right now. Try again tomorrow."

❧

The Good News: You are a better person than you probably think, particularly if you think you could never deal with, say, your parents' senescence if said senescence led you into the world of Depends Undergarments and other unpleasant facts of late life. You can.

Look, I'm a chicken. I speak as one who, going into every squeamish turn, said, "I can't do this," and then did it. I gave showers. I changed adult diapers. If I did it, anybody can. A tip: Buy some medicated VapoRub-type stuff and smear some under your nose when you run into really icky situations. It's the Sandwich Generation's magic mushroom, a Castanedan mind-altering substance.

The Bad News: Even as the physically gross stuff turns out to be less paralyzing than you had feared, the emotional stuff is far trickier, and there is no VapoRub for the soul, unless you count alcohol.

Today, for instance, a hospice nurse and I have to "break" my mother on the subject of nursing homes. First we convene everybody in the living room: Mom, Dad, me, and a few hospice people. We discuss the way the apartment is becoming more and more dangerous. My father wakes in the night and wants to leave the hospital bed we've had trucked in. The only person there is my mother, who cannot support his tottering weight.

We go around the room, soliciting comments about other options, gently steering my parents toward the nursing home.

Each time my father has the floor, he discusses his distaste for the confinement of the hospital bed with its high sides.

"When I want to go to the john, I have to get Barbara to help me, and the whole thing is a nuisance," he complains.

"We don't want you to get out of bed on your own," says a nurse.

Around the room we go, discussing future care options, the likely course of the disease, the advisability of lining up a nursing home placement right now. Back to Dad. Anything else to say?

"Perhaps a ladder could be attached, so that I could climb in and out more easily," he suggests.

"No," I say, "the purpose of the bed is to keep you from getting out and hurting yourself."

He shrugs.

The next time we come back to him, five minutes later, he brings up the bed again, as if it were a fresh topic.

"Bob?" asks the hospice nurse.

"I'd like to say a few words against that bed in there. It's medieval!"

Later, the nurse and I talk quietly with my mother, while Dad sleeps.

"It's the only way. He's not even safe here anymore."

"I can't. I made a Commitment to keep him at home."

"What good will that do if he falls on top of you, and you both get hurt?"

We have to apply just enough pressure so that she can resist, resist, and then cry and give in. She has to be able to blame us for the smashing of the Tablets of Commitment without really having been so mercilessly bullied that there is lasting damage.

When the deed is done, the nurse leaves, and my mother and I are alone with our decision and our patient, who has become endearingly childlike in recent days. No, not childlike, infantile. The realization gives me a little jolt, and I can identify the sense of regret and nostalgia draped over me. It's the ultimate Oedipal joke. My mother and I have a baby. For the last few days we've been feeding and diapering him and trying to discern from his sometimes incoherent pleas what it is he wants or needs. We've been up at all hours. And we're going to miss him when I take him to Hughes Convalescent Home tomorrow.

☙

Hughes is within walking distance from my parents' apartment, so I bundle up my dad, blanket, parka, hood, and wheel him over. The whole thing feels like an afterthought following the Breaking of the Covenant. The people at Hughes greet him as though his arrival were ordained at the hour of his birth. "Oh, there you are!" Big smiles.

They take off the hooded parka and lay him down on a bed.

"I'm Anna," says a beaming nurse.

"I'm Santa," says my father. "But they took away my suit."

"Is he joking or disoriented?" she asks me.

"That's sort of the basic question I've been asking myself for thirty-five years," I tell her.

☙

Every few months, people call up with ideas about what to do with his best play, *The Silver Whistle*. A movie. A TV series. A musical version. It was a Broadway hit for Jose Ferrer about fifty years ago. Then it was a *Mr. Belvedere* movie. Then it was a *Playhouse 90* episode. But producers and agents call all the time to fiddle with new proposals.

I am lost. All of the people strongly connected to the play are now dead or non compos mentis.

I am hunting through my father's files, looking for clues. Here's a folder marked "Theater Correspondences." I am unsurprised to find that only 60 percent of what's in there has anything to do with theater. There are letters of all kinds. All of them are from him. He has saved carbons. I am unsurprised to find that in many, many cases he has not saved the other person's letter back. These would not have interested him as much as his own letter. The letters are funny, troubling, problematic. A person seeking his advice about buying a house or staging a musical was just as likely to get a snootful about William of Orange or the flaws in Trinitarian theology or whatever was on his mind. "There will be a test on Friday," one of these letters concludes.

I am drawn to two. One he sent me in an attempt to patch up a very painful stretch of bitterness between us. It is carefully worded. Admits no real fault. But it eagerly seeks peace. Another is to his agent, who, perplexingly, became a rabbi late in life. The letter brags about me. I am going to give a commencement speech at the private school from which I graduated, it says. Who, it wonders, would have dreamed of such a thing?

෪

With apologies to Thurber, I awaken at 4:00 A.M. to hear, distinctly, a seal barking.

A hunt turns up no seals, just a sick little boy whose virus has turned into something else.

"Sounds like it might be croup," says the doctor on the phone to my wife. "Does he make a sound like a seal barking?"

My dog and father are already sick. My mother is a survivor of recent cancer surgery. My wife has frequent, incapacitating headaches. This, I think in a moment of abject self-pity, is what my life has become. Seal barks and whale songs.

Joey, who is a trouper and notoriously brave about illness, burns in my arms and weakly wheezes out the question intrinsic to every disease.

"Is this going to go away?"

The doctor tells my wife we should take him outside.

Something about the cold doing something to the inflamed and swollen something.

I wrap him in blankets and stagger outdoors with him.

It is January 1998. As an anxious nation holds its breath, Marvin Runyon announces he is quitting as postmaster general to return to the private sector. There is also something going on that has to do with the president and a woman named Lewinsky. I stand outside with a hot child in my arms and tilt my body back so that I can look at the stars sparkling in the cold, black sky. How are we going to get along without Marvin Runyon?

Gazing at the sky, I have a vision of myself, the last healthy person in the world, running from station to station with a bedpan, while the music they used to play for the guy with the plates and the sticks booms out of the clouds. I am in the night sky, a constellation, Sandwichomeda.

When I visit the nursing home, my father is padding around in the halls, moving his wheelchair with waggling shuffles of his feet. In this context he is peculiarly downscaled. He was The Big Show when we cared for him at home. Now he seems like one of several kinds of persons one sees in the halls of nursing homes. The final trick of age and disease has been to make him pretty much like everybody else.

"Can you get me out of here?" he asks.

"No. It doesn't make sense for you to be anywhere else."

He tells me he has been assured I can get him out of there. He also tells me I am, to the best of his knowledge, his father.

My wife succumbs to the Venusian croup-flu. I am now officially the plate-and-stick guy.

Everybody is sick. On a Saturday night I'm leaving alone, to go see *Washington Square,* mainly because I love Jennifer Jason Leigh and never miss her movies.

I'm heading out the door to watch two hours of Henry

James making sure nobody gets anything they really want. Joey asks if I'm coming straight home.

"Where else would I go?" I ask.

"Go out. Get drunk," he suggests.

"And then what?"

"Buy a gun," he adds helpfully.

"Sounds like a great Saturday night. I'm on my way."

⁂

"Who wrote the plays *Macbeth* and *Hamlet*?"

My father thinks a bit. He is sitting in his wheelchair at the nursing home, a place I am starting to like, with its goofy faux-everything, cheery retro-fifties decor. We are in the Bamboo Room, my favorite of the several public spaces, with its poseur Asian motif but no actual bamboo that I can see.

"I don't know," he finally admits. I don't think the whole Francis Bacon controversy is what's slowing him down here.

Maybe multiple choice would be better.

"Who wrote *The Glass Menagerie*? Was it

a. William Shakespeare
b. Tennessee Williams
c. Arthur Miller?"

"*The Glass Menagerie* would be Tennessee Williams," he says very slowly.

I am pleased, and begin again.

"A closed system will nonetheless gradually lose energy. I am describing entropy, which is the second law of

a. Thermodynamics
b. Quantum mechanics
c. Motion."

"That would be motion."

I am sad. He was the one who taught me about the second law of thermodynamics.

"Do you want to keep doing this? I mean, are you enjoying it?"

"Yes," he says.

"Which of the following Revolutionary War generals tried to betray West Point to the British?

a. Israel Putnam
b. Benedict Arnold
c. Horatio Gates?"

A pause.

And then, from somewhere behind me:

"Benedict Arnold!"

Another guy in a wheelchair. He wants to play, too. So we let him. He's pretty clueless about the math stuff.

We move into one of the other public rooms. My mother shows up.

"Who danced with Ginger Rogers?" I ask.

"That guy," my dad says.

"I know 'that guy.' What is his name?" I sing a few bars of "Let's Face the Music and Dance."

Now a whole bunch of people in wheelchairs are beaming at me. They like this game. "That guy!" I could get used to this. Magister Ludi of the demented.

I sing some more. Everybody beams. Everybody is happy. How can we not be? There may be trouble ahead, but how can we not be happy while there's music and moonlight and love and romance? Life, in this frozen moment, is paralyzed with goodness.

"Who wrote *David Copperfield*?"
"David Copperfield."
"What do you mean?"
"I mean that David Copperfield wrote *David Copperfield*."
"That is incorrect. I'll give you three choices.

a. Victor Hugo.
b. Charles Dickens
c. James Polk."

"Why don't we make it Charles Polk?"
"Why don't we?"

❧

My father has a fever.

❧

I start getting calls in the afternoon during my daily radio show. He's bad, he's worse. Should I come now? Not yet, but maybe soon.

Suddenly, the producer gets on the studio monitor and says, "They think you should come now."

I rip the headphones off my head, run to the garage, kick the tires, and light the fires. I'm there in minutes. And he's slipping.

If you've read this, you know I'm involved. You know I've been a good son, pushing the wheelchair, taking care. But I suddenly realize I never said the basic, rock-bottom stuff. My mom leaves the room for a few minutes and I hunch forward and chatter. He is rolling in the sleep of near-death.

"You were a great dad. I was always proud to be your son." Can I really be saying these things for the first time? "You taught me so much, about how to be kind and funny and how to write. I love you. You're a great dad."

He rolls and turns. I think he's hearing. Oh, God, let him be hearing.

My mom comes back in. I sing a few songs, just to have my voice in his ears. We tell him that rest and peace are coming. I tell him he can let go. And when it comes, it comes as a mere slowing down into nothing. No rattle. No spirit flying out.

If he were here, he would know what to say. He would say something funny.

"Death is overrated." Maybe that.

We walk outside. It's night, and the sky is full of stars and a slivered moon. Is this where I'm supposed to look for him now?

The Silver Whistle is about a con man who restores youth to people in a nursing home.

"When you were a child you responded to the wind. To the flight of a scarlet bird at sundown. To the first rays of light across a sea at dawn," the con man tells a woman. "Look up at the stars. Look up at the night. Let the feel of the earth go through you."

At night, I suddenly want somebody in the God business to come to my house and say something wise to me. I almost don't care what. But no one does. If you don't go to the practices, you can't suit up for the games, apparently.

Alone in my car, I sing the Johnny Mercer song I wanted to sing to him as he died. But I couldn't. My voice would never have held, just as it doesn't hold now. It's the one about the two drifters, off to see the world. Suddenly I'm a little kid in the car with my dad, two drifters, off to the zoo or the railroad tracks to watch trains, or to find out what's waiting 'round the bend. Suddenly I'm a middle-aged man crying very hard in a '95 Honda, stopped at a red light on a Friday night in the winter.

❧

He starts to talk to me.

So much is unsaid. So many questions linger. I dig through

his old scripts, as if they were instruction manuals for a suddenly comatose machine.

WILLIE BURKE
[*Smiling as he pours beer*]
It was a grand funeral.

SNOWBIRD TOOMEY
It had dignity, and that's what a funeral needs
more than anything else.

WILLIE
I thought the casket would be heavier.

SNOWBIRD
We were on the end that was up when we carried
it down the church stairs. Then there was the
grade down to the grave. We were on the up end
there too. One of the secrets of living an easy
life is to always be on the up end.

I see that, like any good Irishman, Dad had been preparing
the world for his death for about fifty-three years. He was the
funniest person I ever knew. I miss him, shopping for his casket.
He would have been hilarious. The guy at Taylor & Modeen is
incredibly nice, never pressures us, leaves us alone in the show-
room so I can help my mom spend the right amount. Tight with
a dollar when it comes to the comforts of life, she displays an
unexpected high-roller streak when it comes to the casket. I'm
trying to picture my father in this discussion of wood vs. metal
and of various "interiors." There's nobody home in a dead body,
and you might as well be piling books and bingo games and bicy-
cle pumps on those expensive satin sheets in there. But casket-
shopping touches our inner Egyptian.

When my time comes, burn me up and scatter me in the
woods. I've always known that. But I get a little sucked into the

comfort angle. We find a box that, even I admit, looks pretty cozy. Something about the sky blue interior is deeply inviting and beckons to me, just a little.

"Now, you had brought a dark suit for him to wear, right?" the guy asks.

"Yup."

"See, that's all going to pull together once he's in there."

Oh, Dad. We should have gone casket-shopping ages ago. You would have been a riot.

Burial will be private, but my mother wants to see him one more time, all made up and in the box.

So does Joey.

"I couldn't go see him in the nursing home because I was so sick. Now I want to say goodbye," he tells me.

He wants to give him a toy or something else to keep in the casket, too.

In my mother's kitchen, he spots a type of chocolate cookie my father loved. Dad and my mother fought about them, because his diabetes made them a hazard, the way he went at them.

"You could put some of those cookies in the casket," he tells her. "Bob loved them."

"Oh, no," says my mother, who risked her health and maybe her life to keep him at home until the final ten days, who ministered to him with a tenderness that touched and surprised me. "He's not getting any cookies."

❧

Passing through the kitchen during the day, I come upon a doodle by Joey. He has drawn two Saint-Exupéry stars with arrows reaching up to them. The arrows stretch out from the words

Bob
Oh Bob

Shall we gather at the casket?

Apparently so. I thought nobody would want a "viewing," but apparently everybody does. My mother, wife, and son are at the funeral home looking at the body. So is my dad's cousin Peggy, the closest thing he ever had to a sibling. The mortician, trying to be helpful, has put so much terra-cotta makeup on my dad that he looks like a clay model of himself. All of the hawklike comical ferocity is gone from his features.

Joey has chosen two toys—a stuffed sheep and a plastic fairy—to put in the casket with his grandfather. He has also written a note.

Dear Bob
I love you
If you read this.
Love, Joey.

We're a family of notes, apparently.

When my grandmother died, she left instructions requesting a pair of warm socks and a certain robe she had been saving for the journey to the next life. When somebody went looking in her closet, they found a likely robe. In the pocket was a note. It read, "This is it."

She was my mother's mother, Alma Cotton, daughter of a widowed farm laborer. Standing at my father's casket, I'm dimly aware that I don't even know the name of his mother, whom he could not bring himself to discuss. I know nothing, save one or two tiny details, about her life. I couldn't even guess where she's buried.

On my way to the graveside ceremony, in the brief stretch of road from my mother's apartment to the cemetery, I am seized by an impulse. I want balloons.

I stop at a store, race in, get five blue helium balloons

yoked together with metallic ribbons. Why five, why blue, I couldn't say.

And thence to the cemetery, where a tiny knot of "immediate family" has gathered for a ceremony presided over by Sean Kennelly.

"Joey, do you know Grampa's not in there?" Sean asks, nodding at the box before he begins. ("No," I think giggily, "but hum a few bars and we'll fake it.")

Joey nods yes, and Sean says a bit more about that in his Dublin brogue. He reads a few things, including a bit from a Jewish service, and leads us in the Lord's Prayer. (Who can it hurt?)

And then Joey and I go up on a rise of earth, and he turns loose the balloons. Still tethered together, the blue globes circle one another, weaving, passing through, bobbing, changing places like dancers in some very complex gavotte. Whirl, loop, circle back in the chaotic breezes of noon.

Bob.

Oh Bob.

All of the elements of the man, I think, are drifting into heaven's vault. His love, his humor, his sorrow, his anger, and his fifth element—that remarkable knack for leaving the world and entering magical realms. We can see, too, the silver lightning flashes of ribbon snaking among the balloons.

"Bye, Dad," I hear myself say.

The others keep watching, but I turn away, because my eyes aren't good. And because I'm done. I saw him go up.

Joey, however, is glancing over at the grave, where the casket is still seated in its frame, above ground.

"When do they put it in?" he whispers.

"Not until we leave, I guess."

"Ask them!"

I ask the funeral-home guy.

"Most people like us to wait until they've gone," he says.

"I don't believe this," Joey says.

"Mom?" I ask.

"I don't want to see that," she says.

"Maybe you better get in the car," I tell her.

Joey and my wife, Thona, and I go back to the grave, and the guy lets Joey turn the handle that lowers the whole rig. We watch it go all the way down. Then Joey pulls two flowers, white and red, from the floral piece and tosses them in on top of the box.

"Bye, Bob," he says quickly and runs to the car.

❧

I have to go back to the nursing home to gather my father's personal effects.

The people there are, I've decided, strangely beautiful. They drift slowly through the halls like ships, broken-masted or hull-pierced, never to sail again, but bobbing and eddying in the last harbor, sad and lovely fragments of their old selves.

I pick up a little thread of my father, too. To find a missing thing, you go to the last place you had it.

The *New York Times* runs a generous obituary, written by Rick Lyman:

> Robert E. McEnroe, who wrote *The Silver Whistle,* a frequently revived 1948 Broadway comedy about a garrulous tramp who spreads good cheer through a home for the aged, died on Feb. 6 at the Hughes Convalescent Home in West Hartford, Conn. He was 82.
>
> Mr. McEnroe had written a dozen plays in his spare time while working in the research department at United Aircraft in Hartford before he drew attention in 1947 by selling two in one day to different Broadway producers, an unusual feat for an unproduced playwright.

The obit tracks the history of *The Silver Whistle* as play, television play, and movie. It notes the actors who have played the lead role (Jose Ferrer, John Carradine, Lloyd Nolan, Eddie Albert, and, in the movie adaptation, Clifton Webb), and touches upon the fact that the other play, *Mulligan's Snug*, was never produced "though it passed through a succession of producers who more than once announced plans to open it on Broadway."

The obituary mentions *Donnybrook!*, Dad's short-lived Broadway musical of 1961 that starred Eddie Foy Jr., Susan Johnson, and Art Lund.

It concludes, "Of the years he tried to teach himself playwriting in his spare time, Mr. McEnroe once said: 'I wrote twelve plays in ten years without earning a penny more than my factory wages. The only thing this proves is that it's nice to have a job, no matter what.' "

⌘

Edward, Joey's guinea pig, is sick. Joey and I race with Edward to a small animal hospital in Kensington.

In the car Joey says, "Well, if Edward dies, he'll get to see Bob."

Jeez.

The woman at the desk doesn't want us to be there at all. She has a stern manner, and I get the feeling that somewhere not far from where I stand there is a pipeline backed up with wheezing ferrets, rheumy parakeets, tortoises with hacking coughs. A staggering parade of zoological bit players for whom God's Great Plan did not, originally, include healthcare.

Shamelessly, I play my big card.

"Look, my father died a week ago. This is my son's guinea pig. And he was close to his grandfather. My son, I mean, not the guinea pig. And, you know? I just can't do another funeral."

She takes Edward and promises the doctor will see him "after hours."

෫෫

There's an Italian saying, "Green winter, full graveyard." Edward, a fellow of infinite jest, of excellent fancy, has died. Death plays encores.

Even though Edward was, in Darwinian terms, capicola, I find his death saddens me—monumentally.

I remember another February day, when Joey was six, when he and I went together for the first time to the Bronx Zoo. It was a Wednesday, silver-bright sky and spring-warm air. Somewhere among the Ten Great Days of My Life lives that afternoon, walking my little boy around the zoo in that merciful warmth, doing something my father liked to do with me. What I remember also was that he would not leave until we had found some cousin of Edward. We did eventually locate the cavy—actually what a guinea pig is—in the rodent house, and it struck me as odd that Joey insisted on seeing, in such an exotic place, something he could see every day. But it was important, I finally grasped, for Joey to establish that there, in the firmament of lions and apes and zebras and cobras, Edward had a place.

So Edward's death is not the kind of news I can deliver on the phone. Feeling like a Shakespeare walk-on [*Enter MESSENGER*], I drive to my mother's house, where my son is spending the day.

[*MESSENGER delivers sad tidings. Business.*]

"Well, we knew he was sick. And they don't live that long anyway. If he were in the wild, he'd be dead."

This is Joey talking, not me. He's stealing all my lines. He is often analytical when he doesn't trust himself to be sad. He never cries over Edward or Bob. I wonder whether it is because he is strong and secure or because he has a secret, darkened architecture, a labyrinth of baffles through which he bounces his sorrows. I honestly can't tell, and it seems to me that both could somehow be true.

We are Sims again. Empty and yet so vulnerable that a sick guinea pig could polish us off.

HAMLET
Has this fellow no feeling for his business,
that he sings at grave-making?

HORATIO
Custom hath made it in him a property of easi-
ness.

HAMLET
'Tis e'en so: the hand of little employment hath
the daintier sense.

Thonk. Thonk. "Gwine see Miss Liza!" I try a bit of singing at grave-making, but the dirt will not budge. "Gwine go to Mississippi!" It has been a green winter, but beneath the green, the earth is hard and resentful.

Edward will lie in state (in the garage) until I can figure out how to dig a hole.

I look up from all my troubles and see that Joey has been, in a funny way, neglected. He has the pasty, sunken-eyed look of a boy who has spent too much time alone with Nintendo.

So we take a hike up Rattlesnake Mountain in Farmington, Connecticut, on a cold day. It's a good place for us to go and drop our burdens and get more connected to rock and sky. We have used the mountain in this way all our lives together.

Joey likes to dramatize a hike by falling deliberately from time to time. He is on the ground from one of these falls when Roy, our old, old dog either fails to see him in time or simply cannot, because of arthritis, manage to miss him. Roy steps on Joey's face, leaving a muddy pawprint on his cheek.

Joey finds this interesting.

"Now," he says, "I know how the ground feels."

Maybe that's my next job. Get myself oriented. Know how the ground feels.

≈❦

After Bob dies, I discover that I have joined, willy-nilly, the Dead Fathers Society, the multitudes of other men who have been clobbered in their forties when their fathers died.

What you see, in guy after guy, is a sense of wounded surprise. They didn't know. They didn't anticipate the lists of unspoken truths and unanswered questions that would sprout, fast as June radishes, in the space where their fathers once stood.

I get letters from men who say they are still, after twelve years, in some kind of dialogue with the shades of the departed dad. The acceptable obsolescence of fathers is deceptive advertising. "He's big. He's tough. He's stoic. You won't mind when he croaks." Humbug.

The guys in the DFS soften their voices when they tell you their stories. It's our secret handshake, this bruised little voice.

It hurts and goes numb, hurts and goes numb. There are days when I want him around, for a dose of his odd politics, let's say. And there are harder days when I want to confess the secrets of my life to him and ask him how I should live from now on.

But it's never really bad, because Dad and I had all that time. I don't regret a walk or a song or a diaper or a quiz question. I could have done a lot more, but I did enough. Enough to show him love and give me peace. That's all you can ask for.

If you're lucky, now and then, you get more. You get something that feels like grace. Maybe you get a spot on the up end.

He is dead, and there are one million unspoken words. We were estranged for a lot of those years—not exactly enemies but wary men, brushing past each other, as empty as Sims, as guarded as ghosts. I sit down again with his old scripts, turn the pages. Absurdly, he starts talking to me again—this time about the afterlife.

[*Two knocks*]

                    SNOWBIRD TOOMEY
It's him.

                    WILLIE BURKE
Is that you, Dennis?
     [*Two knocks*]
Does two knocks mean yes?
     [*Two knocks*]

                    SNOWBIRD
Wait a minute. Two knocks could mean no. In that
case, when you asked him if two knocks meant
yes, he could have knocked twice for no.

                    WILLIE
     [*Annoyed*]
Dennis, what's no?
     [*One knock*]
What's yes?
     [*Two knocks*]
     [*To Toomey*]
I hope you're satisfied.

                    SNOWBIRD
Are you in hell, Dennis?
     [*Two knocks*]

Do you feel miserable?
  [*One knock*]
Do you feel bereft and forlorn?
  [*One knock*]
Do you feel repentant?
  [*One knock*]
Is your spirit in deep despair?
  [*One knock*]
Do you yearn for alcohol and women?
  [*Two knocks*]
Do you yearn for poker and racehorses?
  [*Two knocks*]
Is there any point in our praying for you?
  [*One knock*]

WILLIE

  [*Beams*]
He's fine. He's fine.

Two

Why Nobody Understands Turbulence

"When they asked you to write this book, I have a feeling they were picturing a more normal family."
—Thona McEnroe

Sarah Whitman Hooker Pies recommended with this chapter

- ◆ Captain Jim's Live Pigeon Pie with shotgun
- ◆ Mary Beth's No-Filling Pie for People Who Don't Trust Anybody
- ◆ Mabel's Date Nut Marshmallow Goo
- ◆ The Green Bastard

We scroll back twenty-two years. In July 1976, my father goes walking in the hot breath of the Connecticut summer and dies.

I get a call at the newspaper where I work. Something is wrong, my mother says. Come home now.

The air has the texture of hot Vaseline. His doctor had told him he ought to take walks for his high blood pressure. His doctor had not thought it necessary to add, "Discontinue walking when the atmosphere around here resembles the inside of a vaporizer."

So he sets out at a nice, brisk clip through the heat and humidity and ambles along until his faculties begin to veer out of whack.

He stumbles into the house and collapses. He may have fainted. His body simply decides that his brain cannot be trusted and temporarily relieves it of command. Ensign Unconsciousness, the bridge is yours. When I arrive on the scene, he has improved, reaching the state of cognitive bleariness that passes, among adult male McEnroes, for normal.

I am twenty-two and need, at that exact moment, to jump into my car and drive without stopping to the Blue Ridge Mountains of Virginia to see a woman. This is not a good time for me to preside over the death of my father.

"He looks fine," I tell my mother.

"I *am* fine," my father calls out from a nearby dimension.

"He's not fine," my mother says.

I look around the room. As usual, I am not 100 percent sure whom we are worried about. I will be making my trip in a very unsafe car. I own a Capri 2000. Things keep breaking off from it. Not the usual things, either, like side mirrors, although one of those has broken off, too. I mean things like seats. The driver's side bucket seat, for no reason at all, breaks off from the floor one day. On a rainy afternoon, as I drive down the road with my wipers slashing furiously back and forth, one whole wiper arm suddenly breaks off and flies out into the downpour. It is as if a person had waved so excitedly that his arm snapped off. The key breaks off in the lock, and for a time I start the car by putting the fat end into the hole so that it meets up with the thin part trapped inside. After about four months, I decide this is unnatural and have a locksmith pull the thin key sliver out. But during its time of living inside there, it strikes some new bargain with the tumblers. My back-up key will no longer start the car. So I take the entire ignition housing off and let the switch dangle down. I start the car with a screwdriver. I leave it parked in crime-infested neighborhoods, but nobody will steal it, either due to or in spite of the fact that the hard work has been done already.

My father, meanwhile, has somehow injured his right arm, so that the one thing he really cannot do is turn a key in an ignition. For the next twenty years, he reaches awkwardly over the steering wheel and starts the car left-handed every time. As the song says, When the world is running down, you make the best of what's still around.

This is during a time when some of us name our cars. I know a woman named Louisa whose decrepit Chevy Nova is named Flattery. Because Flattery will get you nowhere. She stomps the gas pedal and bellows, "Goddamn it, Flattery!"

My car is named Angst.

Anyway, I myself am mildly scared of driving to Virginia in Angst, but then, I am twenty-two and there is this woman. I catch myself wondering if that—combined with what I am hoping to do once I get there—has anything to do with my mother's hysteria.

"He looks fine," I try again.

"He's not well."

"Go," my father says from his mists. "I'm fine."

He doesn't seem worried about my driving Angst all that distance.

"You weren't fine before," says my mother.

"I was influenced . . . by elves." This notion seems to cheer him.

"How bad can this be?" I try.

"Don't be fooled!" my mother answers shrilly. "He's making jokes now, but half an hour ago, he didn't even know his own name."

My father gazes off into the middle distance, as if weighing the merits of that statement. Then he smiles beatifically.

"My name is Claude Rains," he says. "And I am a movie actor."

I laugh. My mother blows up. Angst and I go to Virginia and, implausibly, come back alive. I'm tempted to say that I don't remember anything else from that twenty-six-year-old trip but I would be lying. The young woman and I have missed each other terribly. Her parents are there in the house. We slip out into the Blue Ridge night to embrace on the cool, wet grass. And her brother's border collie finds us immediately. Circles, worries, whines, sniffs. Fusses if we try to shut her back up in the house. We see the black-and-white snout and concerned eyes emerging from the darkness, darting in to meddle with whatever we are doing.

For years, I miss the point of the entire episode, which is not—it turns out—about Claude Rains or heatstroke or any of the forces tugging me toward Virginia or collius interruptus once I get there. Of more lasting importance is the chance remark about elves.

The little people are back.

❧

He's talking to me again.

His old plays swarm with spirits and fairies. I've placed the scripts in a sort of Rubbermaid crypt. It's a big plastic box with a hinged lid and curved top, like a treasure chest, and the plays are restless inside there. All the characters and apparitions and odd-

ities from those musty pages leap against the sides of the crate
like eels in a stewpot. Down, wantons!

MS. EMILY BOGGS
Have you seen anything odd in this house?

WILLIE BURKE
Snowbird saw a gnome.

EMILY
What kind of a gnome?

SNOWBIRD TOOMEY
There aren't kinds of them. A gnome's a gnome.

EMILY
Where was the gnome?

SNOWBIRD
In my room.

EMILY
Did it look evil?

SNOWBIRD
There was no reason at all for it to look evil.

EMILY
How did it look?

SNOWBIRD
[*Thinks for a moment*]
It looked inscrutable.

EMILY
Do you see gnomes all the time?

SNOWBIRD
I do not.

                        EMILY
Frequently?

                       SNOWBIRD
No more than anybody else.

                        EMILY
Everybody sees gnomes?

                       SNOWBIRD
When they're there to see. You can't see a non-
existent gnome.

                        EMILY
Have you been seeing gnomes for a long time?

                       SNOWBIRD
You're twisting things around. I don't see
gnomes. That means you see them where they're
not there. The only time I see gnomes is when
they're actually there to see.

                        WILLIE
Snowbird is very down to earth. You'll never
catch him seeing things that aren't there.

In 1946, my father wrote *Mulligan's Snug,* a play about a
New York City barroom infested with fairies. *Mulligan's Snug*
was optioned eleven times for Broadway but never staged. One
of those eleven optioners showed the script to the eminent
British actor Sir Cedric Hardwicke, who wanted nothing to do
with it because "it's about fairies, and Englishmen don't believe
in fairies."

Irishmen do.

A gentle acquaintance with fairies can make certain troubles—including Englishmen—a lighter burden.

Not that troubles ever become so light as to fly away for

good. And not that fairies can be trusted to act in anyone's behalf but their own.

"You'll never get them little ones to do what you want. They'll do what they like. Minds of their own," says Mulligan, the bar owner.

"Witness the nature of the creatures," writes Yeats himself, "their caprice, their way of being good to the good and evil to the evil, having every charm but conscience. . . . Beings so quickly offended that you must not speak much about them at all, and never call them anything but the 'gentry,' or else *daoine maithe*, which in English means good people, yet so easily pleased, they will do their best to keep misfortune away from you, if you leave a little milk for them on the window-sill over night."

I grew up around fairies, the way some people grow up around horses or Jack Russell terriers or guns or surfboards.

My father's fairies poured back and forth in his life, swept in and sucked out by sloshing tides of alcohol.

The little people. Their promise to my father, in their whirlings, their caperings, was of a magic that would turn his sorrow—the tragedy that began on the day of his birth—into something so cloudy and fey that it would not hurt anymore. They promised pie powder to sprinkle over his bruises.

You can't believe the little bastards.

Fairies are capricious and flighty. In the middle part of his life, they walked out and left him with nothing, no enchanted sword, no book of spells, nothing but the dull ether of the bottle. And in 1970, fairyless and despairing, he played a very dangerous game and almost took the bunch of us down with him. In 1970, he died in a much more serious and frightening manner than this little brush with the heat of July 1976.

But that is a story for later. Or sooner. We'll come to it eventually, as we work backward through time.

☙

In 1976, Bob McEnroe has played his desperate game. We see him returned from Hades and scorched by a refining fire. His hair, prematurely gray since his thirties, is now white as duck down. On his face, more often than not, is a mysterious half-smile, and it takes the ferocity out of those hazel eyes and that raptor's beak of a nose.

One day, with very little fanfare, he puts down his three-pack-a-day unfiltered Fatima and Pall Mall habit and picks up a pipe. After a day or two of finding out he cannot smoke a pipe without inhaling, he puts that down, too. And forty years of constant smoking—an addiction so severe he cannot sit through a movie—end with scarcely a remark from him. When I was in the sixth grade, he tried to help me improve my athletic performance by running with me around the school ballfields at night, after homework was done. He ran with a lit cigarette in his hand. I would look out in the darkness and see its tiny orange light sailing and bobbing eerily through the ink. The fairies watched from the bushes.

Tobacco has no power over him now because almost nothing does.

The old stories are full of men who return, much changed, from a trip to the underworld. And it would probably be more erudite to mention Aeneas or Orpheus, but my father reminds me most of Gandalf in *The Lord of the Rings,* who falls through fire and water to the "uttermost foundations of stone" while battling a terrible monster. When he returns from death, he is different.

His hair is "white as snow in the sunshine," and his eyes are bright and piercing. And Gandalf tells his friends that, indeed, "none of you has any weapon that could harm me now."

Robert E. McEnroe battles his dark, fiery beast in 1970 and comes back now in the thrall of a gentler magic. Few weapons can harm him, including death.

ॐ

He drafts his living will. I reproduce it here.

To my wife, son, doctor, and any relevant wardens, keepers, or turnkeys:

Death must come to all and mine to me. I do not fear death, but dread the thought of living the seventh age of man as a glob of protoplasm connected to tubes which are tied to machines, valves, regulators, blinking lights, and shrill whistles, and where all prognoses are completely negative.

I do not ask those in charge of me to break any laws of God or man, but, if it is possible, I pray that you will pull the plug, throw the circuit breaker, blow the fuse, or pull the main switch. God bless he/she who disconnects the life support. I cannot offer him/her a place in heaven, but I'll fix up something comfortable in hell.

"Do you seriously expect me to go into court with that?" I ask him.

He shrugs. "Put it under your rubber plant," he suggests.

This is one of his favorite images. He genially accuses agents and editors of having placed his scripts under their rubber plants. And he hands me various odd and disturbing things to put under mine, not that I have one.

One day—this is before the living will—he approaches me with a folded piece of lined yellow paper.

"You mustn't show this to anyone," he says.

"Okay," I agree.

"This represents my refutation of Gödel's 'incompleteness theorem.'"

"Okay."

"I want you to put this under your rubber plant, in case I get hit by a bus someday."

"Okay."

"Gödel's 'incompleteness theorem' is probably the most important idea in all of modern higher math, but I think he's wrong. I'm pretty sure I've got it right."

The hubris in this statement is almost incalculable. Gödel's "incompleteness" is, one could argue, almost as important as Einstein's "relativity" or Heisenberg's "uncertainty." (And they're all cousins at the twentieth-century family picnic of throwing up one's hands over the whole question of precise knowledge.) The only difference is that fewer people have heard of Gödel because nobody really cares whether higher math works or not.

Saying you can disprove Gödel is like saying you can prove ice is really air or that outer space is really black velvet draped over an aluminum frame or that *Ulysses* is really the Dublin phone book.

My father is a polymath, a voracious reader, and a grandiose dabbler with crackpot tendencies. He has been reading extensively about higher math and is just the type to conclude that he has imploded one of the pillars of the field. Now he stands before me in his wool dress slacks and the rumpled white dress shirt he wore showing houses the day before and asks me to join him in this delusion.

"That's . . . great," I tell him.

"You can't show it to your friends."

"I'm not sure I'd want to."

He leaves, and I sit there for a while trying to picture myself spilling the beans to my friends: "Hey, Stinky, my dad has cracked Gödel's theorem. What's your dad up to?" Nyah, nyah, nyah.

❧

There is a rule of thumb in the newspaper business. One of my editors used to call it the "Three-Minute Mile Principle." It's almost as important as Gödel's "incompleteness." People show up in newsrooms claiming to have done all kinds of breathtakingly improbable things. Assassinated the premier of Hungary using oven cleaner and margarine. Held prisoner by talking leopards. Spotted Barry Goldwater spreading banana peels on the Chappaquiddick bridge. And if they're telling the truth, you've got a great story. The problem is, they're usually not, and quite often they themselves don't know that they're not. The Three-Minute Mile Principle is a kind of information triage. It says that you can't spend too much of your life checking out all kinds of nutball contentions. If somebody shows up claiming to have run a mile in three minutes, he probably hasn't.

Should there be a corollary that says, "On the other hand, if you don't check out the wildest assertions, you'll miss Watergate; you'll spend your career confirming and reconfirming the dull normal"?

No. We don't need that rule. You go into the newspaper business because you believe or at least hope that the fabulous is sometimes true, that giants do walk the earth, and that the tip about machine-gun-wielding teenaged dropouts forming a secret commune at an abandoned marina on the river is real. You tell your editor you're going to drive down there and check it out, and she says, "Good," because she's the same way. We don't need any reminder to keep a certain dreamy romanticism alive in our work. We had fathers who talked to fairies and who claimed to be secret math geniuses, fathers who took their pre-Christmas paychecks to the racetrack and hoped the kids would remember the year they came back with the best toys ever.

So when it comes to Bob McEnroe vs. Gödel, screw the Three-Minute Mile Principle. Sitting there with that paper in my hand, I really believe he's done it. What choice do I have? One-third of my identity, roughly, is bound up in the belief that this man with the unruly hair and the permanently distracted look, with his head bowed and his eyes sliding over into an unseeable crack in the universe, this man is an overlooked genius.

Without having to be told, I know that he is worried about

piracy. What if someone, somehow, got hold of his proof (or disproof) and claimed it as his or her own? His only hope is to publish it under his own name, but what journal of mathematics is going to listen to a real estate agent and former Broadway playwright with no formal education in higher math (his recent incarceration in a psychiatric facility being very much the cherry on the Crackpot Parfait)? I know also that, in my dad's mind, this mathematical insight is some kind of souvenir from his supernatural travels, a pale flower plucked from a path in the underworld or an elf-cake baked by the little people.

The little people. He stays up late, communing with them and (more than I know) tippling. They're the ones who have him thinking he's a math genius.

He needs to get it set in type, published, so that he can prove he was the first to refute Gödel. But if he approaches anyone with this idea, he'll be dismissed, he knows, as a crank.

"I have a fiendish plan," he tells me one night.

"Oh?"

❧

So what's *your* father up to?

"The bottom rung on most ladders is a cell, a place to lock away those who might do harm if left free to roam. There are different kinds of cells and they make up a ladder of their own. At the top is the luxury cell, which is set aside for dictators, kings, and presidents. This story is concerned with a cell at the very bottom. It holds a naked mental patient. His mind has been in a fugue state for five years. He is incontinent. He is washed by a hose. His food is prepared in chunks like dog food. He cannot be trusted with a knife or fork."

These are some notes by my father for his novel *The Nemo Paradox*.

My father has never been inclined to do harm, but he knows what it is like to wake up from a coma and find his hands and feet tied to the frame of a hospital bed, to have only the dimmest sense of how he arrived there, to have the daunting and exhilarating task of rebuilding his life from a point of implosion.

From this starting point he constructs a novel. He has never written one before, and I'm not even sure he likes them that much. He plunks himself down at the dining table and writes. Late at night, when my mother and I have given up, gone to bed, he's still writing and—I now see—probably drinking.

The plot concerns a man named Henry Nemo, accused of terrible crimes and treated, because of his thundering rages, to a lobotomy. Nemo wakes from surgery with no knowledge of his identity or past. He reconstructs the world ab ovum and when he learns of the accusations, he escapes from a state mental hospital with the intention of finding himself either innocent or guilty.

Henry Nemo is huge and hairy and dirty and horny.

We have temporarily abandoned fairies and taken up, instead, with a giant.

The Nemo Paradox is its own kind of paradox. It is, in places, poetic, charming, funny, cosmic. "God made the universe—a trillion trillion spinning balls of fire. What did he want a universe for?"

It is, in other respects, crude, hostile, and simplistic. It seems unnaturally concerned with sustained erections and sexual prowess. Most of its women characters exhibit odd and disturbing sexual appetites. If your father had written it, it would give you the creeps. You would start to wonder what was running through his mind when he took you to the zoo or played whiffle ball with you. Here is an example of what I mean and—trust me—I've made a point of staying away from the truly vivid, visceral, and viscous.

"She put her feet on the coffee table so that her thigh pressed against me. I did what anybody else would have done and kept right on doing it until she went from 98.6°F to 102°F. At 102°F her pulse was at 180 and her sweater and slacks were in a pile on the floor. Her central nervous system rang her engine room for steam and got it. She started to writhe like a snake on a hot bed of coals. She moaned, trembled, clawed, bit, whispered obscenities in eight languages. Her hips rotated on a vertical axis, while her pelvis boxed the compass. The effect was gyroscopic and tremendously alive."

Yeesh.

His career as a successful Broadway playwright lies fifteen years in the past, but he finds a William Morris agent named Ramona Fallows and courts her.

"Dear Ms. Fallows," he writes, when she has been too long in responding to his second manuscript submission, "I have been trying to think of ways to get *The Nemo Paradox* out from under the rubber plant.

"The proposal I have strikes me as being dubiously arithmetical, but it's all I have.

"I suggest you read the last forty-nine pages, starting at page 181. If you like this material it will mean that, by adding the material you like in the first version to the forty-nine pages, you approve of 77 percent of the novel. (177/230)

"Of course, there are people who are immune to the charms of arithmetic, and lots of people don't go near rubber plants for months."

Three months pass, and he writes her again.

"Dear Ms. Fallows, I dreamed about *The Nemo Paradox*. In my dream the script was under a seven foot rubber plant in the corner of a large waiting room. The script was squashed down by the weight of the tree. Bits of rubber leaf and rubber-tree spores circled the tree with elastic detritus. As I watched, a small boy used the planter as a urinal. I had the feeling that the script had been forgotten—that whoever had put the script under the tree had left the publishing business and gone into real estate.

"There is no particular reason why you should interest

yourself in my dreams. It's just that I haven't got anybody else to tell them to."

I am an adolescent when this is written. If you think he doesn't intend for me to see myself in the small boy pissing on his manuscript, if you think he doesn't intend for me (and the rest of the universe) to sigh at the notion of his having no one to tell his dreams to, if you think he does not intend for me to find this letter someday—well, you should know that he makes three or four copies of it and sprinkles them through his files.

He does more rewrites and contacts her again.

"The book is finished," he writes to Ramona. "It contains:

2 murders
143 grammatical errors
6 acts of intercourse
847 misspellings
1 lesbian relationship
1,131 corrections made with Liquid Paper
6 B & Es
1 unlikely love story."

I am tempted to say that a second unlikely love story ensues—that of Ramona Fallows's affection for my father's ugly-duckling book. It is nearly impossible to like, but she embraces it anyway.

Alas, no one else does, although virtually everyone else agrees the ingredients for a very good novel seem to be moiling around in the book's innards.

"He writes with real humor and sensitivity—rarities both," says one editor in a lengthy letter to Ramona Fallows about why, ultimately, he is not taking the book. There are a lot of these letters, longer and more ambivalent than most rejection notes. Reading them now, I feel a sense of helplessness on my father's behalf, coupled with a slight unease, as if something in these letters might be contagious, as if something might travel from him to me and push my writing one or two degrees south of saleable.

The letters themselves are so full of little apologies and half-compliments and flashes of enthusiasm that they make a kind of blizzard before my father's eyes, obscuring from him the inevitable truth. Nobody is going to buy this book because nobody likes it. I mean "like" the way you like a dog or your best friend Fred, not the way you like Mozart or *Heaven Can Wait*. There's something a little snarly and uncongenial about this novel.

"If only I'd liked this a little better, all of the above, it seems to me it could be cured by rewriting and editing," writes an editor at Random House. "But unfortunately, I simply don't like it well enough to want to undertake the job . . ."

What is not in any of the letters to or from anybody, what is not confessed to Ramona Fallows, what is not detected by any of the dozen or so editors to read the book is this:

Henry Nemo, our family giant, is afflicted by visions and dreams. Like my father, who can't stop thinking in numbers whether he is writing sex scenes or courting Ramona's approval with unwieldy fractions, Henry has integers flying through his head. Odd progressions pop into his mind, shards of memory from his obliterated life. Taken together, these fragments constitute something my father is desperate to preserve between two covers, with a copyright date and a Library of Congress number.

Once *The Nemo Paradox* is published, you see, he plans to inform the world that these fragments, these prions of cognition sloshing around in Nemo's mind, constitute his refutation of Gödel's "incompleteness."

❧

One day at a small family gathering, my father, in a tone of resigned good cheer, tells my future wife, "I have made every mistake that a man can possibly make."

Every family nurses, as part of its oral history, the plot twist of the missed opportunity, the fortune squandered, the unseized chance that would have led to wealth. Everybody has a grandfather who turned down the offer to be fifty-fifty partners with Henry Ford, or who drank and pissed away an enormous sum, picking up checks for ne'er-do-well friends, or who sold land for a pittance, only to see it become part of the Atlantic City boardwalk.

This is the Universal Fiasco, the Edenic fall of every clan. The only families exempted, I suppose, are Rockefellers and Gateses and Buffets, people who cannot plausibly claim to have let prosperity slip away. What do they do for rue? I suppose it sprouts up in other forms.

In my family, the sense of The Fall is more finely grained, worked into every observation like neat's-foot oil into a baseball mitt. We are more fallen than not fallen. Everything has gone wrong, except on those rare, treasured occasions when things have gone right.

My grandfather makes and loses a million dollars in the 1920s. In the fall of 1947, my father does the unthinkable. As an unknown playwright living in a Hartford, Connecticut, boarding house, he sells two different scripts to two different Broadway producers on the same day. The New York papers can't come up with anything to compare it to. My father becomes the hottest new playwright in New York, and then, after 1948, gets exactly one more play produced in the last fifty years of his life.

He does not stop writing plays, mind you. The scripts are heaped up around me now like the skeletons of the conquered. They're sealed up in polythene envelopes and stacked next to the unpublished novels. All of them are invisibly roped together by a winding skein of bad decisions—writing projects refused and calls unreturned. A stint in Hollywood from which he fled, like Lot from Sodom. Errors unrelated to writing. He shrewdly buys a lot on what becomes the most desirable road in desirable

Farmington, Connecticut, and later sells it for exactly what he paid.

"We don't want to make any money on this," he tells my mother, as if that sort of thing could get them a bad reputation.

But mostly, he is wrestling vapor. Something is wrong with his writing, but he cannot see the flaw to fix it.

And me?

I try to be nothing like him, even though I am exactly like him. Like every protagonist from Oedipus to Sleeping Beauty, I am in flight from my destiny. I will do something else, be someone else.

And yet, somehow, when the mists part to reveal me in adult life, who am I? I am dreamy, moody, fond of alcohol, uncomfortable in my own skin, furtive about my emotion. I am a writer. I am Bob McEnroe.

Still, I try to deprive fate of its victory. Where my dad is a grasshopper, I am an ant. He reaped windfalls and threw his money at cars and dinners and outboard motors. I opt for the weekly paycheck, something he disdained all his life. I write for a daily newspaper and then slowly build a modest reputation for writing short humor pieces. Doubleday publishes my first book. It is moderately successful.

I publish another book with Doubleday. One day, a letter arrives from the company. My books are being pulled out of stock. They will—in the tradition of *Batman* villains and *Terminator* robots—be hurled into vats of acid and turned into pulp.

I can save as many as I want of either title by purchasing them at a special author's insider price of 66 cents per copy. I reflect upon this. How much would it cost me to buy a notebook of that many blank pages? More than 66 cents. From a certain standpoint, my writing has actually depressed the value of paper. It is like water damage. I decide not to buy any copies.

Two days later, a royalty statement arrives from my agent.

My royalty statements usually have parentheses around the number. Although not fiscally savvy, I realize this is not a good thing. Parentheses mean you have money that belongs to somebody else. From a theoretical standpoint, I may actually owe Stephen King $7,018.23 for failure to hold up my end of American biblio-commerce.

This statement is different. No parentheses and in their place, chubby numbers betokening financial health! And then I notice the reason. On the literary agency's alphabetical list of clients, I am apparently right next to Shirley MacLaine. This is her royalty statement. I would expect to be dwarfed by Shirley in North America, but this is her statement for Pacific Rim countries. There are places with no written tradition where she sells more books than I do in my own time zone. People buy them and make canoes out of them. Shirley MacLaine is selling more books on the island of Komodo than I am in my own hemisphere. On the other hand, how is Shirley going to feel when she sees all those parentheses in her envelope and realizes she owes King seven large?

Out of such instructive humiliations, I construct a perspective about myself.

I am careful not to swing for the bleachers. I am not going to burn so brightly that I flame out. I am going to control my gift so that it does not betray me. I have my father's wild swings of Irish romanticism, but I keep them in check with my mother's steady, incremental New England puritanism. I am going to avoid the curse of the McEnroe line, right? Unlike my grandfather, unlike my father, I will not be blindsided.

Right? Right?

୧୫

My wife and I cannot conceive a child.

When I discover this, I have reached the age at which my father felt perhaps the first tickle of his half-century writing problems. I am roughly the age of my grandfather when he went from millionaire to debtor.

The curse of the McEnroe line descends on me in a rush of black raven wings, and here is the new shape it takes: There will be no McEnroe line. I am the only son of an only son.

"The purpose of marriage is to bring forth issue," my father said many times as I was growing up.

Now he says nothing.

My wife and I enter the world of fertility medicine, which is somehow both perched on the leading edge of scientific advancement and trapped back in an age when a hunched-over person with a lot of split ends would shake gourds and throw pulverized lizard entrails at you.

For a period of time—our Von Bulow period—I inject my wife with stuff we keep in our refrigerator. It is made from the refined urine of menopausal women. In the early days of its manufacture, the primary source of the urine was—I'm not making this up—Italian nuns, but I'm not sure this is still the case. I remember reading that the Vatican told the nuns to knock it off.

Although the burdens of the treatment fall most heavily upon my wife, I have some interesting moments. I am required to produce specimens of a substance I am not accustomed to sharing with people I haven't at least been out to dinner with.

Sometimes I am permitted to do this at home, sometimes not. On one occasion I am ushered into a standard gynecological examination room, stirrups and all. I am handed a cup and shown the location of the light switch. No magazines. No Marvin Gaye. The specimen I am trying to produce will be combined with the eggs of a hamster, to see whether my sperm have the ability to penetrate an ovum. If I allow myself to think at all about where I am and what I am doing, I will go crazy. If I allow myself to think that the sweaty, sticky, earthy, ecstatically human business of procreation has been infiltrated by sterile vials of refrigerated nun urine, if I allow myself to imagine all those near-sighted, left-handed, manic-depressive hamsters, I will scream.

I emerge from that little room with a saffron container's worth of climactic fluids. I feel that there should be one of those boxes you step up on when you win at the Olympics. There should be martial music of several nations playing.

But infertility is a quieter world than that.

Now it is my turn to wrestle with ghosts. Cancer and compound fractures and cholera are things happening that aren't supposed to happen. Infertility is a thing not happening that's supposed to happen.

Through it all, my father is a sphinx. He says nothing.

He does not say: "The world will be pretty much the same place whether the Edward-Robert-Colin McEnroe line proceeds or not. Adopt if you like. Do nothing if you like. But don't think I'm staying up nights mourning our genotype."

He does not say: "I don't care what it takes. In vitro fertilization, surrogate mothers, beheading your wife, re-mortgaging the house. Keep the line going."

Is he indifferent, terrified, furious, sad, accepting? I have no idea.

But I remember that line of his that came up half a dozen times over the years, usually when we were deep into our philosophical debates about the meaning of life and the nature of society: "The purpose of marriage is to bring forth issue."

❧

The universe abhors an imbalance. Even as I whirl through this travesty of trickling out my seed for the delectation of small tan rodents, my writing career prospers. I get the interest my father wishes he could have from publishers and agents. I become a contributing editor at *Mirabella* magazine for its first two years, and the publication's early buzz begets more offers for me. Where my father is infertile—laboring over manuscripts and then stuffing manila folders full of rejection letters from agents and publishers—I am ripe.

On the other front, he has conquered, and I am vanquished.

It is his birthday. The four McEnroes—my father and mother, my wife and I—are out to dinner, crimped to the table in our usual uneasy state. Three of us have roughly the same capacity for sharing our feelings as the neolithic stone heads on Easter Island. My wife, a psychotherapist, a talker, a prober, a confessor, is the strange new plant growing among us, a poppy shooting up amid pachysandra.

My parents are not relaxed diners. They track the flow of food and staff visits in a kind of mental Domesday Book. Look at those people. They arrived ten minutes after we did. Now they're being served before us. There's an eternal quest for restaurant justice. Tonight, my father is especially restless, although the service is not slow. Where is the waitress? Why hasn't the order come?

"Just relax," I tell him, as gently as I can. "There's no hurry. I mean, do you have somewhere you need to be after this?"

"No, but I want to get there anyway," he says. He grins and snaps his fingers in a parody of himself as guy-on-the-go. He is seventy-two. He'll be going home to stare into the night and watch the little people creep along the edges of the carpet.

There's wine on the table, maybe just enough to move the four planets out of their usual uneasy orbit.

My wife cranes forward out of her chair. She looks at my father. "How do you feel—" The three of us start, as if a cobra had abruptly materialized and begun darting its deadly head at us. "How do you feel . . . ?" What kind of horrible question is this going to be? A how-do-you-feel question, that's what kind. We don't like that kind.

". . . about the fact that we can't have a baby?"

Oh, Jesus.

My father is talking, but, in the custom of our family, not to anyone that we can see. He is looking at a point in the air above the table.

"I think that Thona should get an ax. And a wheel on which to sharpen the ax. And when Colin comes home each evening, she should be sitting at the wheel, sharpening the ax."

"What does that mean?" my wife asks.

"It doesn't mean anything," he says.

She stares at him. I glance at him uneasily. My mother looks at her plate.

That'll teach her to ask how anyone feels.

In the car going home, Thona says, "Did you understand what your father said?"

"It seemed as though he was saying that I needed to be threatened with a sharp ax so that you and I would have sex," I tell her.

"That's what I thought," she says.

Of course, the one thing you do, when you're infertile, is have sex. Not when you feel like it. Not when you're horny or feeling affectionate. But when the cycles and pills and shots demand it. You have sex when you're exhausted or sad or emotionally flatlining. You have it in the missionary position to maximize your chances. Sometimes you're lucky enough to do it when it's fun. But the one thing you don't do is skip it, because that would make all the incisions and scopings, the injections and minor surgeries, the humiliating tests and expensive medicines completely pointless.

Here is my father, a man who sits home and plows through Descartes and nuclear physics. Races through Stephen Hawking's book like it's *Dick and Jane*. Devours history and theology after the rest of the world has turned in for the night. His is the supremely wakeful mind. And this is what he has surmised about his son and daughter-in-law.

He has watched the whole high-tech medical melodrama

unfold, and this is what he extracts from it: an Iron Age *Jiggs and Maggie* scenario, involving sharp blades and sexual coercion.

I am hurt. I am outraged.

A few months later, in the midst of a deep funk about the state of my marriage, my infertility, my weird father, I find myself on the phone to my mother, and to my surprise, in defiance of the McEnroe tribal law, I am talking about it.

"How could he say that to us?"

"I thought it was a strange comment. I don't know what he meant," my mother says.

I tell her what he meant.

"Oh, dear. I'm sure he didn't mean that."

"Well," I say, "he did mean it. What's more, he meant it to hurt me. What's more, he's angry and envious because I have a book deal, and he doesn't. Don't tell him I said that."

So she hangs up and tells him.

A day or so later, a letter arrives from him.

Of course he is proud of me and my book. Yes, it hurts a bit that I seem able to get published so easily. Any writer would envy my current path of ease. Perhaps, he suggests, my current psychiatrist is stirring up things inside me. Psychiatrists have a way of doing that. He himself has spent long stretches on the couch, he reminds me, and knows how seductive the vision of the "new self" is, with its bold new ways of truth-telling and blasts of fresh air blowing out the cobwebs of dormant falsehoods. The difficulty is, he observes, that the people around you are still living their old lives, and they're not necessarily eager to meet the bright new person you are becoming.

Message: We are doing just fine with denial. Don't rock the boat.

Oh, and the hatchet thing?

"Your mother told me about your reaction to a statement I made. I was shocked. I never had any thoughts like those and— if I had had them—I would have kept them to myself."

I put the letter in my desk drawer. The thing is, he has a point. This is not the kind of family where one person can independently decide to start telling the truth. At the time of this letter, I have been his only son for thirty-three years. He has never told me even one story about either one of his parents. I don't even know my grandmother's name or how she died or when. What I know of my grandfather comes only from my mother. My father's paranoia about any probing into his childhood would be appropriate for one of Julius and Ethel Rosenberg's kids. Once, when I asked him what each of his parents died from, he huffily asked me, "Do you have any formal training in psychiatry?"

"No, but . . ."

"Maybe you should leave these kinds of questions to professionals who know how to handle them."

"I was just asking what my grandparents died of. It's the kind of thing that comes up on medical forms."

He was silent for the rest of the night.

On the other side of the family, my mother and her mother did not speak to each other for seven and a half years during the 1970s. I was their go-between. On holidays, I would arrive laden with gifts from my mother to her mother, with instructions to pretend they were from me. Boxes and boxes, which my grandmother would open slowly, as if her own daughter might leap out of one of them, like a spring snake from a gag candy jar.

"Barbara shouldn't buy me so many things," she would say wistfully.

The fight had been about me, about a speeding ticket I'd gotten, but not really. It was truly a long, wordless wail, a lonely wolf call about change and loss. What these New England women do is harden, like the rocky, frozen soil they grew up on. Their hearts, their arteries, their positions, their resolve, even their visages. The proper response to every scarcity, every injury of time, is to harden. That's why they call it hardship. My mother ended the drought by simply showing up at her mother's door unannounced (and dragging me along, of course). The two began chatting as if no bitter, silent interval had ever occurred.

"Do you have any idea how weird that was?" I asked my mother in the car on the way home.

"We're Yankee women. That's how we do things," she said, as if the manual for this had been written in 1681 and handed down from Increase Mather.

No, denial is not something our family can give up the way you give up butter and switch to margarine.

❧

Maybe this is a good time to talk about the Court of Pie Powder. To say nothing of the lists of pies that begin each chapter.

My father never knew it, but his McEnroe forebears came from the tiny Irish village of Mountnugent, in the south of County Cavan, northwest of Dublin. I didn't know it either until after his death, when I started work on this book. I began to wonder how I got into this messy business of being who I am, and eventually it seemed as if the only thing to do was go back to Ireland and ask people. I found our people in Mountnugent. You'll meet them later in the book.

Wondering how Mountnugent—it doesn't sound very Irish—came to be, I drove up north to the city of Cavan and clawed around in some research materials. I discovered the granting, in 1762, of letters patent to one Robert Nugent. This meant that the British were willing to let Nugent treat his area as a village, with two yearly fairs and a weekly market and "a Court of Pie Powder and all customs and tolls."

A Court of Pie Powder, it turns out, is not as nice as it sounds. I suppose you could say the same about a lot of places. The term is a corruption of the Norman "Pie Poudreur" or "dusty foot." The Court of Pie Powder meted out rough justice, especially to peddlers and vagrants.

We could make it into something nice, you and I. There aren't any Courts of Pie Powder anymore, so we could make it mean what we like.

It struck me, anyway, that a Court of Pie Powder could be something I've been searching for all my life. We are, most of us, jammed with grievances and guilt. We are filled with suspicions of ourselves and others. I suppose some people are not, but you just want to strangle them. Who couldn't use a Court of Pie Powder, where one's life is gently kneaded into a pliable mass and then rolled out into a fragrant oval, pressed with skillful, floured fingers against the bottom and sides of a pan? It's nice to be kneaded.

The proceedings of a Court of Pie Powder would be less concerned with guilt or innocence or liability or malfeasance and more concerned with sweetness and mouthfeel. Life is messy and so are pies. The best you can hope for is to set the whole overheated shebang to cool on the sill for a few decades. The court would be more about tortes and less about torts. It would be a chance to sift, to mix, to trim the excess and flute the edges of a troubling existence. It would be a way of having desserts that are better than our just deserts.

The Court of Pie Powder is a fine place in which to treat my father, who once idly invented a pie company as a way of distracting himself from the long afternoons he spent in real estate offices, not selling enough houses. His was called the Sarah Whitman Hooker Pie Company, and the name was based on an actual Revolutionary War heroine who had lived near where we lived. She housed imprisoned British officers at her home and somehow managed to charge them money for it, I think. That was her heroic feat. It's the kind of upper(pie)crust Yankee moneygrubbing that still plays very well among your New England higher orders.

The Sarah Whitman Hooker Pie Company—"Try a Hooker for a Change!"—suffered a little bit from a *Playboy's Party Jokes* sensibility, but some of the pies were memorable. The pies that I mention at the start of each chapter are his ideas.

Col. Ellwood's Sensible Peach for Young Christian Women
Glutton's Pie with Oscillating Bottom and Crispy Handles
Hamlet Pie with Egglet and Toastlet
Mango Mango Bang

There were dozens more. I used to look at the lists of imaginary pies and half-wonder whether he shouldn't be spending a little more time trying to earn a living.

The Court of Pie Powder would be a place for dismissing exactly that kind of a charge in a milky, dreamy, Sendak Night Kitchen setting. When I catch myself feeling bitter or resentful of my dad these days, I picture us both in the floury haze of the Court of Pie Powder, acquitting ourselves.

We acquit ourselves pretty well.

❧

Through the comforting white fog of pie powder, I look back to that time of infertility and his devastating hatchet remark and see Bob McEnroe in a different light.

He is frightened. He is sad. "I have made every mistake that a man can possibly make." He cannot persuade the spark of his writing to jump its gap. With each new day, he is more memorable as a peculiar man—full of intellectual quirks—who works in a real estate office, and less persuasive as a young lion of Broadway, the man who went out to Hollywood and fended off stars who hoped he would write a play for them. He doesn't even tell those stories. Patricia Neal, Kirk Douglas, Elizabeth Taylor rapping on his door, asking to meet with him. Who would believe it?

And now his son has a problem. He can't help. And he's not exactly untouched by all this. Here in his early seventies, he is thinking about what remains behind and what goes forward, after he dies. The McEnroe DNA double helix isn't whirring like an eggbeater, burrowing into the future. It's bunched in a knot, tumbling across the floor, getting kicked around with the dust bunnies. In fear and frustration, he lashes out with a weird remark whose meaning he himself barely grasps.

Case dismissed.

❧

For the last forty years of his life, he sits in a series of real estate offices, dreaming of pies, often selling very little real estate but engaging in other, feverish activities. He wears a jacket and tie every day and looks, alternatingly, down at the floor and off into the ether. This habit of not looking at people is one I have, alas, inherited. He cannot remember anybody's name, ever. I can remember names with almost archival precision but have no idea whom they belong to—I cannot recognize faces. There is even a name for this: prosopagnosia or "face-blindness." (Imagine the size of the name tags at the Prosopagnosia National Convention.)

He requires "personal space" at least as big as a Major League on-deck circle, and the women who work with him make a little game of backing him in skittering arcs around the room simply by taking one step closer every time he steps back.

The older he gets, the more his feverish mental activities interfere with the selling of real estate. He is almost incapable of dealing with customers whose interests are, in his view, limited—that is, people who seem mainly interested in either buying or selling a house.

If people are willing to discourse with him about the Hundred Years' War or the fact that hippo jaws can easily crush a boat or how many of the twelve billion neurons in the human brain are firing at any given moment—if they are any fun to talk to during those long stretches of driving around in his car—he might be able to help them buy or sell a house.

Mostly, though, he is doing a different kind of work—assembling some kind of Grand McEnroe Unified Theory of Everything.

When he dies I inherit a series of late-in-life appointment books, in which startlingly few appointments are recorded but whose every page is crammed to the margins with observations and musings. They are like the notebooks of some modern-day Lucretius, if Lucretius had recorded, with equal faithfulness, (*a*) insights into the nature of things, (*b*) work he did on his Ford Escort, and (*c*) what he had for lunch and dinner (especially if Lucretius had chicken croquettes quite often).

There are passages and pictures clipped from magazines and pasted to blot out whole afternoons and evenings, and bits of rumination: "God created the universe. He set a hundred billion balls spinning in space that may be infinite. Most balls had no life or points of interest. A few balls delighted God, and he kept track of them. Our ball grew lizards and God liked to watch the big lizards eat."

The appointment books sometimes seem intended for consumption by some outside party. There are even instructions. "Unfold," it reads on the outside of a folded-up clipping about Tennessee Williams that is pasted into a page. Whom is he instructing? Me?

These and other items in the Robert E. McEnroe Archives have a way of hitting me, from time to time, with bolts of unpleasant lightning. Some of the entries are about me—I am seen as stinting, unforthcoming, bordering on unkind—and some are painful in other, unexpected ways. I have learned to peer into all this clutter the way one watches the last reel of *The Silence of the Lambs*, peeking through parted fingers with one's hands in front of one's eyes.

Here is his appointment book for 1989. I am playing posthumous detective, snooping around for some clue to his mood about adoption. I am scanning the weeks surrounding October 1. He has meticulously recorded problems with my mother's car and the fact that he had chipped beef for dinner and, on one occasion, something called "reinforced soup." He has carefully written that Reno, Nevada, is west of Los Angeles and has noted a few facts about *Griswold v. Connecticut,* the landmark birth control decision. He has filled many blank lines with names. Names of people he once knew. Names of characters who appear in his scripts and names he intends to give future characters. Songs he remembers and shreds of ideas. Actors he worked with. "Gaffer Doyle." "Grilled Cheese." "Eddie Foy." "Let Me Call You Sweetheart." "Father Finucane." "Rubber Ducks." "Glazed Chicken." "Kitty O'Shea Craemer." "Colin." "Georgia O'Keefe." "Welsh rarebit."

Where is Joey's birth?

He has noted that an owl is "a flat-faced bastard." Or maybe that is something you would call an owl if you wanted to hurt its feelings. He has written, "Eddie has the piles." There is no one in his life named Eddie, except his father, who is forty years dead. Maybe he likes the sound of it.

On October 10, he has written, "M. I. L. died 12:25 this day. She was a good woman."

I stare at these initials for weeks before I realize that they stand for mother-in-law. My grandmother, Alma Cotton, who did not speak to her own daughter all those years.

She was the one who wrote the note about the robe, when death was far away but near enough. My grandmother could see it striding toward her, like a Sunday afternoon visitor, walking from a great distance down flat farm roads. "Just take me to Windsorville," began the note. There was a little cemetery there and a place next to her husband, who had died about fifty years ahead of her. She wanted a robe and heavy wool socks.

"I intend to be comfortable if there is such a thing in the next world," she wrote.

On October 5, I find, "Foster grandson born. Will be picked up in Texas late in October." He hasn't, as you can see, figured out the difference between "foster" and "adoptive." He hasn't, as of this date, offered even a whisper of support or promised me he will love this child or told me that, whatever I need, he'll be there for me. Because he has no idea whether that's true or not.

And then, on October 23, at the bottom of a long column that starts with "Unicorn Couple" (don't ask me) and continues through "Pork Chops, Louise Gabyson" and "Randy Kolodney," I find "Joe McEnroe."

❧

In October 1989, Thona and I fly out of Hartford in a thunderstorm.

We land in El Paso, and roughly forty-seven seconds later—or so it seems—someone hands us a baby. We must spend part of a week in the city, waiting for various approvals. We meet with the baby's birth mother, who is tiny and beautiful. She is from Juarez, Mexico. She asks us only one thing: "Teach him to love himself."

One evening, we begin to run out of formula and diapers. I leave the hotel and walk through the city to find some. El Paso is a place where possibility and fate mingle in the air and lie on the skin. It's the borderland, a place where, as Gloria Anzaldúa once wrote, "the Third World grates against the first and bleeds."

It is October 21, 1989. At a stoplight where the traffic backs up, I see a Mexican woman moving slowly from car to car. Slung over her shoulder is a baby, about the size of Joey. In her hand is a paper cup from a fast-food place. She is collecting money, wordlessly. I give her a little. A soft "gracias" floats back over the traffic.

I am seized by the way tiny shards of chance erupt into cathedrals of destiny, the way flecks of happenstance adhere and accrete into the crystalline structures of life. Where is that other baby going? To what life am I taking Joey? And how does the difference happen?

"Teach him to love himself." I'm not exactly the expert on this subject. If she knew the family history, she'd grab the baby back. I can't even promise that his new grandparents will acknowledge him. Why couldn't she have said something easy, like, "Teach him quantum mechanics"?

Much later, when Joey is eleven and feeling awkward and miserable, Thona tells him the story again, the story of his birth mother saying, "Teach him to love himself."

"That's working out great," he says dryly.

Walking back through El Paso with the diapers and formula, I struggle to remember a Pablo Neruda poem that describes all these portentous feelings, but I'm no good with poems. Me trying to come up with an apt poem is like Spinal Tap trying to harmonize at Elvis's grave.

I look it up when I get back. It's called "Let's Wait."

Other days to come
are rising like bread

or waiting like chairs or a
pharmacopeia, or merchandise:
a factory of days in the making:
artisans of the soul
are building and weighing and
preparing
days bitter or precious
that will knock on your door in due time
to award you an orange
or murder you in cold blood where you stand

This is how life feels all of a sudden. My grandmother dies. My son is born. Fate is whacking me with a croquet mallet.

When Thona and I return from Texas with the baby, my parents come to our house and sit on our creaking, sagging redwood deck. It is a warm day for mid-autumn. We have a big yard, loaded with oaks and maples. The leaves are yellow. The baby's skin is the color of coffee with milk. My mother holds the baby, and my father holds back.

The baby's eyes flash with brown intensity.

What the hell is going on here? the baby wonders.

A few weeks later, we leave Joey alone with his grandparents and go out for the night. They play with the baby for a little while, and then it is time to put him to bed in his port-a-crib.

My mother retires to a separate room to let the baby settle into sleep.

My father tries, but he can't.

Because . . . what if . . .

He goes back in the room and sits down on the floor, next to the port-a-crib.

And he stays there for maybe a couple of hours, watching the shadows of sleep steal over the tiny form in the terrycloth pajamas, watching the little head turn in slumber.

Because . . . what if . . .

He's hooked. He will spend the remaining years of his life as Joey's shaman, the high priest of a religion for two, an alternative world of cassette players, compasses, calculators, goggles, hammers, pulleys, socket wrenches, wristwatches with peculiar features, binoculars.

The appointment books make space on their orderly lines for a new presence. Joey's arrivals and departures, naps, tantrums, and exclamations are charted along with everything else.

I enter my parents' apartment one afternoon. Joey is three. My father's nineteen calculators and eleven wristwatches are competing for space with Joey's action figures, which may or may not include Spiderman, Captain Hook, the Little Mermaid, Recession Man, Mr. Suppository Head, McNeil and Lehrer, Bobo the Penguin Boy, and Jack Kemp. Two insane collections are at war.

My father is staring fixedly at Joey and holding up a cassette case.

"Mr. Dwarf," he says very seriously, "do you remember where you put what goes inside this?"

In time, stranger devices will emerge from his Dr. Caligari's Cabinet.

"Do you think he is old enough to have his own knife?" my father asks me.

"His own *what*? He's five years old!"

"Just a very small knife."

"No!"

When Joey is eight, I enter the apartment one day to find my mother panicking, my father flummoxed, Joey laughing and yelling, "It wasn't me!" My father has somehow obtained a version of the device used to foil bank robbers by squirting indelible dye all over their ill-gotten gains. He has, in the course of showing it to Joey, accidentally triggered it, and green oobleck is spurting into the room.

"Dad!" I yell.

"Bob!" my mother yells.

"It wasn't me!"

❧

"Because . . . what if . . ." I am my father in that way, too. In those early days, I, too, cannot keep myself away from Joey as he sleeps. I develop a manic obsession with whether or not he's breathing. He often breathes so quietly in his sleep that I need dead silence to hear him. I need to hold my own breath, to get rid of that competing sound. I need to bend low, close to his little head, with my own breath forming an anvil in my lungs and my blood turning into steel bands around my temples . . . just one more second . . . can't breathe yet . . . haven't heard baby breathe . . . And then I have to dive out into the hallway and *pluuhhhhhh* exhale noisily, take another breath, and go back in because . . . what if . . .

One night, when Joey is four, I am putting him to bed.

What I do not know at this moment is that, earlier in the day, my wife, while dropping off Joey with my parents, noticed a plastic toy gorilla and launched into an impromptu explanation of evolution.

She then departed, giving my parents a chance to add their own thoughts.

I know none of this, so I am startled when Joey says, "You know Barbara [my mother] doesn't come from monkeys."

"She doesn't?"

"No. I come from monkeys. And Bob comes from monkeys, but Barbara doesn't." He is quite serious about this.

"What," I ask, already dreading the answer, "does Barbara come from?"

"Pilgrims."

"I see."

"Why are you laughing?"

"Go to sleep."

It might be the ultimate sign of acceptance (and price of admission) into their world. They start telling you preposterous lies. They're going to make him a crazy person, too, like the rest of us.

❧

Joey makes Bob happy. He says quite openly that the idea of living a long time holds a new allure. He's got a grandson. The idea of an Irish line abruptly turning Mexican has begun to amuse him. He's got little people. He's starting to write about them again. He doesn't feel especially good. He's drinking a lot, mostly secretly. He refuses to make a connection between those two things.

He writes:

Dear Colin and Thona,

The partial script I am turning over to you does not require any of Colin's time. This is good because he doesn't seem to have any time. This raises the question: Why submit a script? For what?

For some time, Barbara has been loading me down with major diseases. The number of diseases run from one to five, depending on her mindset. Her chief concern is liver disease because the patient dies in agony. She perks right up when she gets to the agony part. One goes out screaming and thrashing at the pillows. People at the bedside put cotton in their ears and do their beads. I am in the market for a motorized wheelchair with a claxon horn and a place to hide a gin bottle.

Fogarty's Folly is a rewrite of *Mulligan's Snug*, which was optioned by eleven Broadway producers but never got on a stage . . .

If I die tomorrow look for *Fogarty* material in my yellow pads. If I don't write it all, Colin can put his name on the script along with mine. This presumes that he doesn't hire another writer to finish the script.

Now let me give you the nasty part. I have no intention of dying until I am 125. That means Colin will be eighty-six years old when he gets the script.

Pere

He dies five years later of cirrhosis.

The letter is not exactly brimming with trust in me, is it?

❧

What kind of son does not even know of his father's deadly drinking? I did not. I lived in the same town. I saw him once a week, at least.

Both he and my mom are adept at masking symptoms and behaviors.

My mother knows all the basic neurological field tests—

reciting the presidents in reverse order, counting backward by sevens—and she practices them. So she'll pass. Because if she passes, there won't be anything wrong with her.

"Barbara's goal is to have Alzheimer's and to have nobody know it," my father says.

His goal is to drink himself to death before anyone can intervene. If you see elves in your sober hours, how will anyone know when you're lit?

He talks to me now.

On the pages of the old scripts, there's a kind of Tippler's Creed. Here is what he wrote, even as his liver was dying from drink. Denial gets a bad rap, but in the hands of a master . . . well, read on.

MS. EMILY BOGGS
God help you both. Your minds are rum-soaked, gin-soaked, whiskey-soaked, wine-soaked and beer-soaked. Your livers would frighten first-year medical students.

WILLIE BURKE
We've got the best livers in town.

SNOWBIRD TOOMEY
Everything inside us is under control: hearts, lungs, kidneys, small intestines, large intestines, white corpuscles, red corpuscles.

WILLIE
We are completely protected against ill-health.

SNOWBIRD
The only way you can kill us is with a gun, knife or rope.

EMILY
Neither one of you looks healthy.

                          WILLIE

You're looking at the outside. The outside has
been struck by ice storms, snow storms, rain,
hail, cold wind, hot wind, soaps, lathers,
razors, aftershave lotions and wet kisses.
That's the outside. It's the inside that we're
talking about. We take the Patrick Finnegan
Holistic Help for Bartenders and Potato Famine
Fighters.
     [*Takes out pill bottle*]
It's in capsule form. Patrick Finnegan's Pills
for Men Who Dare.

                        SNOWBIRD

Turn it on the side and read the label.
     [*To Emily*]
Wait until you hear this.

                          WILLIE

B_1, B_2, B_3, B_5, B_6, B_{10}, B_{11}, B_{12}, B_{13}, B_{15},
PABA, choline, inositol, A, D, E, F, G, H, K,
L, M, P, T, plus 14 minerals.

                        SNOWBIRD

You have to be careful not to use too much or
you'll lose your taste for alcohol.

                          WILLIE

It's a delicate balance.

                          EMILY

What about cirrhosis of the liver?

                        SNOWBIRD

That's all taken care of by the B complex group
and folic acid.

EMILY

Heavy drinkers have a high mortality rate.

WILLIE

You're right. One hundred percent of heavy drinkers die. The question is, when do they die and does alcohol shorten life or prolong it?

SNOWBIRD

Alcohol is hard on filter-passing germs. And if a germ can't get through the filter, it has no chance at all. Alcohol will kill it dead.

WILLIE

Every time there's an epidemic, the teetotalers go belly-up by the thousands, while drinking men carry on the world's work.

❧

He accumulates thirty-five or forty pocket calculators.

He buys them obsessively and requests them as presents. The slightest new wrinkle in trigonometric function is enough to make him want the latest model. After his death, pulled from various cubbyholes and tumbling out of cabinets and heaped together, they look rather demented, as if he had been striving to count something uncountable.

"Hewlett Packard has come out with a pocket calculator that costs $300," he writes in a letter to me. "I dream about it when the moon is full."

That same letter, typical of his correspondences, offers the following insights.

"Remember, for the first 325 years, Christianity was Unitarian."

And

"When Werner Heisenberg was on his deathbed, he said

that he had two questions to ask God: 'Why relativity?' and 'Why turbulence?' Werner claimed that God would be able to answer the first question but not the second. Science doesn't understand turbulence; neither do engineers, but they have to deal with it."

And

"Twenty-nine years from now there will be 10.6 billion people on earth."

The letter concludes with a paragraph speculating on the case of William Kennedy Smith, whom my father adjudged "a lying bastard." I refuse to quote any of the rest of it here, because it's full of sticky sexual mechanics, the kind of thing a normal seventy-year-old father would be unlikely to share with his thirty-seven-year-old son.

He isn't trying to shock or perturb me, I know. He likes to work on publicized criminal cases and considers his judgments on all of them to be final. There isn't any way to work on the Smith rape case without getting into such matters as semen production, apparently.

The thing is, I never *asked* for information on the Smith case. Or turbulence. Or Christianity. These are not part of any dialogue. Just things he thinks I should know.

❧

Here is a birthday card I have saved. It came to me in the mail about ten years ago, probably when I was turning thirty-seven.

On the outside of the card is a vase of white tulips and a Bible lying open to a page marked with a white ribbon.

"God Bless You on your birthday," it reads.

The inside begins with a quote from Psalms: "The earth is full of the goodness of the Lord."

Then it reads, "Wishing you a bright and beautiful birthday . . . a day alive with promise, rich with possibilities, filled with the wonder of God's love for you."

Underneath that, in red ballpoint, my father has scratched:

Just stay out of hell please.

Pere

☙

A most peculiar man. An irresistible man. Our offices are fifteen minutes away from each other. I drop in a lot. He is almost invariably there, especially in those later years when he is less likely to be showing houses. I find I need him. He is never going to put his arm around me and offer up one of those "Well, son . . ." sessions that seem to happen mostly in insurance commercials. In fact, he is most likely to cut off all conversation by brandishing some kind of horribly difficult quiz he has spent the morning devising. I need him anyway. He is never boring, and even if he were, it wouldn't matter. He's my father. The man who talks to elves.

The fanciful world of Bob McEnroe starts to rub off on Joey.

When Joey is three, we walk in the woods pretending to be Robin Hood and Little John. I tend to get the sidekick roles.

"I am somewhat afraid," I say as dusk steals over the forest. "What if the Sheriff of Nottingham and his men come upon us?"

"I have my sword," he informs me soberly, "and you have your humble staff."

When he is four, Robin Hood gives way to Hawkeye from *The Last of the Mohicans*. So now I am Uncas, the brother. We are scrambling over some rocks in coastal Maine, role-playing. But the rocks are a little perilous and the fall to the water is sheer and long. I become nervous and ask him to move away from the edge. He points to a breathtakingly dangerous series of outcroppings twenty-five feet over a place where waves crash up against the bottom of a cliff.

"We must go there."

I put my moccasin down. No. We absolutely cannot go

there. It is an unnecessary risk, and even brave Indians did not take unnecessary risks, because they were in it for the long haul and understood that Nature deserves a healthy respect, etc., etc.

He lets me finish and then says, slowly, evenly, "Hawkeye would take a chance. To save a life."

Next it is Batman.

"Let's walk the dogs in the spooky woods in the dark," I suggest, one crisp autumn night.

"Only if we wear costumes," he counters.

"What kind?"

"Batman and Robin."

"Fair enough."

We extract costumes from his slightly disturbing collection. There's a pretty good Batman ensemble—cowl and cape—that fits me. He gets some Robin stuff. We drive over to the creepy woods and walk down into them, but even with the costumes and even with the dark, protective bulk of Roy, we don't feel very safe or stay very long.

Back in the car, he notices that I do not appear to be driving us home.

"Where are we going?"

"Gotta return some videos."

"We're dressed up as Batman and Robin."

"Shouldn't be a problem."

"I'm taking my stuff off."

"That's your business."

"Are you going in the store with your Batman stuff on?"

"That's my business."

"I'm staying in the car while you go in."

"You can't. It's not safe. What if something saw us in the woods and followed us? What if it's waiting for you to be alone in the car?"

We enter the store and he veers sharply away from me, hugging the outer walls.

In cape and cowl, I saunter over to the counter and return the videos.

"Everything quiet tonight?" I ask the crew in blue and gold.

"Yes, Batman."

"No unusual behavior or disturbances?"

"No, Batman."

"Very well. You know where to find me if anything crops up."

"Yes, Batman. Thank you."

I leave, followed at a reasonable distance by a small scurrying form.

"I kind of like being Batman," I tell him, back in the car.

"Where's your Batmobile? Batman doesn't drive around in a dumb Honda."

Little boys grow up hopping from hero to hero, like rocks at a river crossing. Next are the X-Men, Luke Skywalker, and after that, Bruce Willis in the *Die Hard* movies. Now it's Harry Potter and Frodo and Legolas.

Champion follows champion until one day I find myself at the reservoir, with my father, watching Joey ride his bike.

Jesus, they don't give us much time here, do they?

☙❧

The clouds are wolf-gray and roiling with overdue rain.

"It's going to rain this afternoon," I tell Joey. "Maybe we should go see a movie."

Joey is six. This will be our first trip ever up Rattlesnake Mountain. In the years to come we will climb it hundreds of times, sometimes with friends, sometimes with Thona, but often alone, just the two of us, trying to get close enough to the sky to work something out. On summer days, he and his friends will walk around the upper ridges, wearing fuzzy caterpillars on their chests, like a fruit salad of military decoration. On one ill-advised winter ascent, I will tie dog leashes to his waist and lower him down icy ledges. On gusty March days we will crouch in the lee

of boulders hearing the wind blast around us and puzzling silent-
ly over our own problems.

On our first climb, it is November 1. It looks to me like
rain.

"It won't rain," he says simply. "We can climb."

He is never wrong about the weather, so up we go to search
for the cave of Will Warren, "a sheep-stealer and Sabbath-breaker"
from the early 1800s, according to the local histories. I stuff
some Halloween candy and water into a knapsack, and we clamber up through brush and bittersweet and dried milkweed, past
radio towers and into eerie, dense woods.

When we come to a stretch of dubious handholds and pre-
cipitous toeholds, Joe lights up. Uncas's spidery ascent, his vain,
heroic quest to save the hapless Alice, is alive in his mind.

"You are Uncas, and I am Hawkeye," he tells me once or
twice. He has said it so many times, on so many hikes, that it is
almost an incantation. Today, I search his voice for a new, sour
taste, but I don't find one. This is good. We have been struggling
over his behavior, and there have been some nasty scenes that
left cracks in the perfect egg of our love for each other. He had
been watching a videotape of *The Last of the Mohicans,* the
Daniel Day-Lewis version, which is probably too violent for cultural anthropologists in their twenties, let alone small boys. So
I'd hide it. He'd find it. I'd hide it better, and Thona would help
him find it. (She liked it, too.) Finally I smashed it with a ham-
mer, which was a brutish and silly way to solve the problem.

"I don't mind," he said calmly when I did it.

I don't mind. It's what you say to the Hurons to show them
you are strong.

Afterward, he fished the tape from the wastebasket and
inspected it carefully, as if its guts held some clue to the magic.
I felt like a stupid, awkward father, and I wondered if he would
ever forgive me. I come from a land, as you will see, where
things can go deeply, irreparably wrong.

We come to a deep gray rock formation and haul ourselves up and down ledges, real Uncas stuff. We eat Kit Kats on a flat expanse bumping up against gray, burgeoning clouds.

We feel the cave before we see it. I do, anyway. The outer rock is no different from the rest of the mountainside, but all through the woods around it there's a low hum, fraught, ominous.

The entrance is a cervical gash at ground level. We crawl on our bellies to get in. The sheep-stealer and Sabbath-breaker spent his days reliving and reversing his own birth, apparently.

We linger for minutes only, running a flashlight beam around the walls. But we're both jittery, and happy enough to get out.

On the hike back, there are some places where he asks that I take his hand as we work down a steep grade. Most of the time, he resists help.

"Dad," he says, apropos of nothing, everything, "you are my partner forever."

Benediction.

Three

Bliss

Sarah Whitman Hooker Pies recommended
with this chapter

- ◆ Anne Louise's No-Filling Pies for people
  who are not hungry, who don't trust anybody, who never get anything right

- ◆ We do not recommend pizza pie

❧

This is the first time my father died. It is 1967. The demons and
dark places are getting the upper hand, and my family has drift-
ed from being a charmingly quirky folie à trois to a rogue unit
capable of some truly disturbing backcountry operations.

The first hint I get of the strange days to come is a sudden
move out of the West Hartford neighborhood where I have
grown up, where I have lived for twelve of my thirteen years. My
parents have fallen into a dispute with the management of our
apartment complex. It is never clear to me what the cause is or

who is truly in the wrong, but there is a rather ominous visit from a Hartford county sheriff, serving papers.

My mother sits me down one day.

"We're moving to Newington. It's just one town away. You can't tell anyone about this. Nobody. None of your friends," she says.

These are dire circumstances, she explains, and we face terrible calamity if our plans are revealed. From the look on her ashen face and the stricken tone of her voice, you might conclude that we are fleeing Nazi Germany with minutes to spare before the Gestapo raps at our door.

She convinces me. I have a circle of about a dozen close friends in the neighborhood, boys with whom I have shared all the adventures of childhood for more than a decade. I tell none of them. The moving van arrives during the day. The next time they come to look for me, I no longer live there.

ॐ

I never spoke a word to any of them ever again. I don't even know, to this day, who came to knock on my door or how the news of my disappearance spread. I was too ashamed to attempt any explanation or to contact them at all later, and, as the years passed, I developed a quiet, perverse pride in having pulled such a gigantic stunt.

It strikes me now that my mother succeeded, unintentionally, in re-creating a peculiar quirk of her own childhood. She grew up in Dana, Massachusetts, one of four towns flooded to create the Quabbin Reservoir. Her entire childhood lies underwater now. My grandmother told me of taking a canoe out on the lake and looking down to see foundations and even the occasional hitching post. It was sort of like life imitating Freud, who understood water, in dreams, to symbolize the unconscious.

My childhood now lay in the murky depths alongside hers. I had been tugged loose from it, like a berry from a bramble.

Somebody should have stopped this from happening. Somebody should have made sure I told my friends I was moving or, failing that, helped me patch things up with them afterward. No one seems to have even thought about it. My mother was far too wrapped up in her housing battle, and my father . . . The obvious candidate was my father, but I have almost no memory of him from the time of the West Hartford exodus. He was, it turned out, drifting down through his own murky depths, although it would be several years before we discovered how deep and dark his abyss was and what kinds of monsters lived there.

There are no photographs of us from this period. The Leica and Roloflex cameras with which my parents documented my early childhood were packed away now. There were no pictures taken of us as a family—or even of any two of us—for about nine years. Some kind of enormous vanishing act was underway.

※

We move to an apartment in an enormous house on Main Street, in the adjacent town of Newington. If one of Freud's patients had dragged this house out of the haze of a dream and onto the analysis couch, Freud would have said it was a metaphor for fragmentation, for dissociative states. The house is chopped up into five apartments. There is an older couple, Holocaust survivors; a middle-aged woman living with her "nephew," who later turns out to have been, instead, her lover; an apartment full of stewardesses; and the Cristinas, a young couple with a baby.

Our landlord is a pale, thin, dark-haired man named Werner. He is a Christian and extraordinarily fond of blowtorches. These two facts are probably unrelated, but I get them entwined in my head from the very start. As we move in, he is still tuning up the apartment, and from time to time I find him lying on the floor, immersed in a project. He might murmur something half-heartedly evangelistic about his church just as I notice that the hissing near my calf is not the serpent from Eden but acetylene. Sometimes I find several blowtorches going, in different rooms. It makes me wonder about the nature of services at Werner's tabernacle.

Our apartment is very nice, with a fireplaced living room, a big, airy kitchen, a downstairs master bedroom and, upstairs, two bedrooms. I live by myself in this upstairs space. There is a door I can close at the foot of the stairs if I want even more isolation. And isolation is the leitmotif of these years. I know nobody in Newington and am not about to meet anyone, because by now I am enrolled at the Kingswood School, a West Hartford private day school where I will be from the seventh to twelfth grades. I am the Guy Burgess of my old neighborhood—living out my exile in a cold foreign capital—and even my new friends from Kingswood are discouraged from coming to see me by my parents, who dislike visitors.

We live in Werner's house for five or six years, and during that time no friend from my age group ever visits those two upstairs rooms. In fact, almost nobody ever goes up there except me. It is the kind of setup that might make you worry that your kid is up there dropping acid or addicting himself to snuff pornography. I am not. I am not even masturbating or listening to the Mothers of Invention. I am just getting kind of nonspecifically weird.

One winter, I send away for one of those massively complex games—Strat-O-Matic used to lead this field—that allow the player to simulate professional sports contests using dice and elaborate paperwork and charts rating the strengths and weaknesses of the real athletes. I assume that Nintendo and its cousins have now obliterated this entire genre, but it enjoyed a heyday among reclusive sports fans. Mine is based on the NBA, but I quickly see that it is not idiosyncratic enough for the kind of crackpot I am becoming. I adapt it and invent my own imaginary professional basketball league, populated by fictional characters, a sprinkling of real pros, and even some college players who aren't going to make it to the pros. I actually—the Hinckleyesque quality of this alarms me in retrospect—take to writing to the coaches of obscure college basketball programs at places like Murray State in beautiful Murray, Kentucky, and asking for the annual guide issued by each team, with write-ups on all the players, some of whom I absorb into my game.

Persons familiar with Robert Coover's novel *The Universal Baseball Association, J. Henry Waugh, Proprietor* will imagine the jolt of unhappy recognition I get when I read it years later and see myself in Coover's drab, lonely, vaguely hallucinatory protagonist.

For company upstairs, I have the Cristinas. Werner did his own remodeling, and when it came time to close up old doorways that had connected sections of the house, he simply fitted a piece of plywood into the space and painted it the color of the passageway. About a half-inch of cheap wood separates part of my upstairs Colinworld from the young Cristina family.

The Cristinas fight a lot, which is kind of interesting, but they eventually grow more conscious of the nearness of me because they move their quarrels to another room. Norman Cristina, who looks like a more compact version of Tommy Smothers with just a hint of swagger, is an avid volunteer fireman and becomes a minor celebrity in Newington because, on two occasions, he happens upon fires and brings them under control single-handedly.

This was bound to appeal to my father, who is utterly insane on the subject of fires and fire equipment—so much so that he is incapable of watching fire trucks pass his car without following them, no matter who else is in the car or where we thought we were headed. Many a drive is disrupted with a U-turn and the high-speed pursuit of a hook and ladder while my mother shouts "Bob!"

So he and Norman hit it off a little, and he is quite disappointed—but also, I think, darkly amused—when Norman is arrested for setting the fires he had discovered and extinguished. More fights and then the Cristinas move out.

᪥

There are fights in our house, too.

I never join them but I hear them. My father's anger—as black as boiling pitch—is oozing across his heart, claiming larger hunks of him, extinguishing the gentle fairy-light of his humor as surely as Norman Cristina would put out those fake fires. It has been six or seven years since he's had anything produced. He spends most of his days at a real estate agency, and his nights writing after my mother and I go to sleep. From time to time, he gets a call from someone in his misty past, someone who wants him to write, oh, patter for a Barbra Streisand one-woman revue, and he dismisses that person with a snarl and a withering remark.

Is he really even writing, by this time?

I have a letter, written by him in 1976, to the William Morris agent named Ramona Fallows. It announces a sort of comeback, in the form of *The Nemo Paradox*, the dark novel that emerges from this period. "I quit writing in 1967," it says. "This is the only thing I've written since."

Can this be true? My memories of life at home with my parents are of an unbroken blur of yellow pads etched with the sharp black lightning of my father's handwriting. Coming downstairs in the morning, you would find two or three of these pads scattered around, the work of nocturnal spirits. It seems impossible that at any point this stops, but perhaps it does.

Certainly the unsuccessful scripts are piling up around the edges of our life like snowdrifts against a door. *The Ears of the Wolf, The Exorcism, The Rettinger Case,* the much-rewritten *Mulligan's Snug.* Producers option them, and sometimes bring them close to production. Directors are hired and casting begins.

And then, poof, something happens, and my father is back home, his head drooping a bit.

"What's your father doing? How's his writing going?"

I get so I dread the questions. I feel tired and compromised from having to lay out all these elaborate stories of "not quite." "Not quite" is the one that got away, and that's the world's favorite example of a wheedling narrative, one that seeks glory with nothing material to shore it up.

And then something worse happens. The questions stop coming. Six, seven, eight years go by with nothing by Bob McEnroe in production. Nobody thinks of him as a writer anymore. He is an eccentric real estate agent who, at one time, had written.

So my job changes. I become the last true believer, the person who brings up the very subject I had once dreaded. My father, he's a writer!

A few people remember. Among them are the Mark Twain Masquers, a Hartford amateur company whose members lionize him. Their chief patroness, a wealthy woman named Sunny Roberts, arranges to fund a scholarship for me at Kingswood, mainly out of admiration for him. And during this period, they decide to resurrect and stage *The Silver Whistle*, his undisputed masterpiece.

For a different sort of person, this could be the proverbial shot in the arm, a little pep rally to remind him of who he is. For him, it merely deepens the sense that his writing is ill-starred, is now remanded into the custody of unpaid hacks.

They lure him to a few rehearsals, and he comes home each time in a mild dudgeon, telling me, "They're going to butcher it."

On opening night, he goes to the theater, makes his way backstage, speaks encouragingly to the cast.

And then goes home.

"What are you doing here?" I say when he appears in the living room.

"I'm not going to watch that."

"What if they announce during the curtain call that the playwright is here in the audience and asked to stand up?"

"They'll be mistaken."

∾❧

If in fact he stopped writing around 1967, then his last play from that period is *The Exorcism,* a dark comedy he researched and wrote before William Peter Blatty's *The Exorcist* was published.

It is the story of Willie Burke, a man in his twenties who believes he is possessed.

Willie's father is Martin, charming, funny, drunk, prone to failure, self-important, foolish. We first see Martin entering the house after a night of tippling in a bar. Sadie, a spinster relation who lives in the house, catches him.

MARTIN BURKE

[*Bowing*]
Martin Burke at your service; friend to man and beast; kind to trees, flowers, rock and common clay.

This is the play that most strongly feels as though my father is speaking to me from some distant reach of time. It's the instruction manual for Robert E. McEnroe. I'm a little late in realizing that.

Martin is the play's comic relief. He is married to Bessie Burke, "a bony, horse-faced woman who wears a pince-nez pinned to her dress" and who conducts séances in her parlor. She is stern. She is commanding. She is cold. She is, except for the séances, every inch the woman my father rarely mentioned and never discussed, the woman so invisible in my life (and yet so much the author of it) that when I began this book, I realized I did not know her name. She is his mother. My grandmother. Or so I believe.

The play is a slow burn at this woman, Bessie Burke. The anger is papered over by Martin's fey humor, some of the best comic writing my father ever did, and rather close to the bone for the McEnroes.

Here is a scene in which Willie's psychiatrist visits the house to learn more about the family history.

MARTIN BURKE

Insanity? There's been no insanity in my family. The Burkes have always been a sound people . . . and dependable. The Burkes have always been a dependable people.

CUTLER

No insanity?

MARTIN

None at all. The nearest thing there was to it was an uncle of mine, Snowy Dougherty, who acted a little odd. In fact, they put him away from time to time . . . just to keep him from hurting himself.

CUTLER

He was suicidal?

MARTIN

No, indeed. Snowy liked life too much for that. He had spells come over him where he'd do things to himself with pins and needles and razor blades. He was harmless, but when he got that way he'd talk about beheading women and it used to make the women nervous. That's why when he got that way the women would insist that he be locked up. He didn't mind very much. He was an amiable man who kept his emotions under control. If he'd been quiet about beheading people, he'd never have been locked up at all.

                    CUTLER
He sounds like an unusual man.

                    MARTIN
     [*Indignant*]
Snowy Dougherty was as fine a man as ever walked the earth.

                    CUTLER
Was there anybody else who acted odd?

                    MARTIN
My grandmother killed herself but there was nothing odd about that except the way that she did it.

                    CUTLER
How did she do it?

                    MARTIN
     [*Shakes his head*]
I'd rather not say how she did it.

                    CUTLER
You can tell me. I'm a psychiatrist.

                    MARTIN
That's no reason for telling you, and I won't.

                    CUTLER
But . . .

MARTIN

The woman did herself in in her own way. If it
was unique, it was because she was an unusual
woman. If it was a little weird and gruesome, it
was because the woman was upset at the time.

CUTLER

It's rather important that I know how she did
it.

MARTIN

It's not important at all. If I thought it was
important, I'd tell you.
   [Snorts]
If it's the queer ones you're after, they're all
on the wife's side of the family.

Insanity, suicide, the fierce comedy of self-delusion among
the Irish. This play should have been distributed to our congre-
gation of three. By 1970, it would be our book of common
prayer, our liturgy, our order of worship.

🙰

Outside Werner's house, America is going crazy, but very
little of 1968 penetrates our world. We could be in one of Edith
Wharton's novels. Or one of Ray Bradbury's. I don't have Tommy
Smith and John Carlos posters on my bedroom wall and I have
only the vaguest sense of Abbie Hoffman.

At school there is a sense of the unfolding moment, but it
is cushioned by all the energy a private school expends on making 1968 look as much as possible like 1948 and 1928. We wear
jackets and ties every day, assemble in a chapel each morning,
and regard girls as speculative, like purely theoretical astrophys-
ical entities. There is revolution in the air, but it is filtered to a
thin mist by the time it reaches us.

A new teacher arrives in 1968. His name is Tyler C. Tingley, and he had attended the school himself. Now he is fresh out of Harvard and brimming with idealism. He teaches my ninth grade English class, where he is alternately worshipped and tortured, depending on which sensibility prevails in the ranks that day. On torture days the class responds to his candor and thoughtfulness with fusillades of cynical, hostile remarks. They research his personal life and history as a student and cunningly weave the new information into their hurtful taunts. Of particular interest is his wife, Marcia, who is beautiful in a luminous and detached way that reminds me of Yoko Ono. How does this earnest nerd of a teacher merit the desirable Marcia? my classmates wonder.

I don't join in the torment, or at least I'm not comfortable carrying it beyond the gentle teasing Tyler seems to enjoy. I need him. He is the first teacher to applaud my writing, to push me beyond mere workman-like schoolboy prose. He singles out a short story I have written from the perspective of a lizard and makes sure it is published in the school literary magazine, which is called *The Wyvern*. Wyverns are English dragons, and everything at Kingswood is a Wyvern, including the teams. It doesn't occur to me until later to wonder what my father, so radicalized an Irishman, thought of this school drenched in faux English heraldry.

What does he think, for that matter, when four young Englishmen become my new gods? One day Tyler Tingley arrives in class with, of all things, Beatles albums. Did we know, he asks, that Beatles lyrics often contain hidden messages, disguised references to all sorts of things? We do not. I certainly don't. I haven't been paying a great deal of attention to the Beatles, and the idea, in general, that pop music is about anything grander or deeper than cars, girls, and sunshine is contrary to my understanding.

We begin to study *Revolver* and *Sgt. Pepper's Lonely*

Hearts Club Band, with Tyler prodding us along. What is the Albert Hall and why would you try to fill it with holes? Who is kicking Edgar Allen Poe and why? The more we dig, the more we find.

"Sometimes," Tyler tells us, "John Lennon seems to stick images in there more for his own amusement than because they convey something important. Another writer who did this was James Joyce. Some of the excitement in interpreting work like this is solving all the little mysteries. Which are the important ones and which are just a writer being playful?"

Boom. It is as if someone has tossed a hand grenade into our midst. We become mavens for literary exegesis, detectives of symbolism and—especially in my case—maniacal Beatles scholars.

Almost every boy in the class is, in some sense or another, converted, but a few of the meaner cynics find it difficult to admit to themselves that this nerd, this weenie, has swept such powerful ideas into our heads. They step up their taunts and, following an earnest explanation by Tyler of what is meant by the term "lay reader," one of them—the angriest boy among us— waits until Tyler is out of the room and scribbles, on the board, "Is Marcia a lay reader?"

This has, at long last, the sought-after effect of making Tyler C. Tingley lose his composure.

"I come in here and I try to treat you like grown-up human beings, and what I get is the chance to find filthy things written about my wife," he shouts.

The tirade continues from there. I am ashamed for all of us, and a little bit fearful that somehow the covenant between him and us has been broken. I can see that Tyler is, more than any- thing, hurt, and coming from a family where emotions are bat- tened down and stowed in watertight holds, I have no idea how serious an eruption like this might be. Perhaps he is so wounded that he won't be taking us on any more journeys into unimagined mental realms.

No, a few days pass and everything is just fine. Better, in fact. The bullying stops, and the magical mystery tours resume. Here in the world outside my family, it is possible to clear the air.

The next fall, the world is suddenly seized by the notion that Paul McCartney has died. Partakers of this fallacy turn to Beatles lyrics with an exegetical scrutiny that would have put tenured Joyce scholars to shame. I am seized by the mania. It is my first exposure to the delightful shade of paranoia that attaches itself to a possible conspiracy loaded with clues and virtually empty of consequence for oneself.

The headmaster, Robert A. Lazear, occasionally summons me to his side at lunch for a briefing. He is amused by the whole thing, and I have a kind of feverish, anal-retentive earnestness that makes it, I'm sure, even funnier.

Paul is, of course, not dead, but, lacking any common sense, I have no way of knowing that. Or maybe I sense Death's bony hand reaching into the center of my world and feel a little safer projecting the subject onto a risk-free canvas. So I scour the earth for motes of Thanatos and ignore the beam under the beams of my own roof.

The real walrus picks me up in the afternoons, roaring up the long driveway at Kingswood in his maroon Impala station wagon as if the Furies were chasing him. It is a standing quip among the students. Watch out—here comes McEnroe's old man.

❧

His drinking intensifies. There's a joke I've heard Jews tell about themselves: Why don't Jews drink? Because it dulls the pain. That's exactly why and how my father does drink. When he drinks martinis, he bolts them in one gulp and sits back, waiting for the anesthetic. I never see him savor a drink, never see him use liquor much differently than a soldier in a Civil War field hospital would use it, although my dad's wounds are all emotional. But he rarely drinks a lot in public, at least not during my lifetime.

The exception is this period. Suddenly, he is out in the evening, drinking. He hits cars and other stationary objects with his car. There is an arrest, a night in jail.

He invites me into the Impala after that one and apologizes.

"You should never have to go through anything like that," he says abjectly.

It seems to me that I hadn't gone through anything. He is the one who had gone through something. I hadn't even gone to the police station to retrieve him. And something that happened off premises is, by definition, a break from his saturnine, snappish brooding. I don't say any of this.

But a few months' time brings the Great Pizza Incident, and then it doesn't matter what I said.

ॐ

More from *The Exorcism*:

MARTIN BURKE
[*Stands and raises his glass as one who
is making a toast*]
To all the poor bastards who slip quietly down
into their basements to get away from nagging
women, I bring hope. Martin Burke has put on his
spurs and picked up his whip. Whittle on your
wood, men, bang with your hammers, cut with your
saws, make little holes with your drills. The
birds need the birdhouses. But have courage,
take heart. Burke is going to ride—for himself
and for all of you. Don't cringe when the cellar

door opens. Don't panic at the sound of light footsteps on the cellar stairs. When the old lady confronts you, pick up a hatchet and tell her that Burke is riding and a hundred thousand bloomers will feel the crop. Tell her that you're a man and that you deserve respect. Do that for Martin Burke, and he'll do the rest for you.

    [*Bows*]

God bless you all.

    [*Crosses to stairs*]

I must rejoin my regiment.

    [*Goes off stairs*]

BESSIE BURKE

    [*To Sadie*]

Please go up and see that he doesn't go to bed with his shoes on.

SADIE

He's wearing spurs tonight, and they'll rip the hell out of the sheets.

Pizza is a wonderful thing, but it has become terrifying in our house because of the way the pies are cut in the Hartford suburbs.

The pizza parlor, instead of cutting the large pie into long, tapering triangles, creates trapezoidal pieces with crusts along the perimeter and then, in the middle of the circle, a cluster of pieces that have no crusts. I have come to think of those as "filets," although at the time of our troubles, I am incapable of irony about pizza, incapable, really, of any attitude save gnawing fear.

My mother takes the position that

1. the filets are intensely desirable, and that
2. the way to preserve order is to create a social compact that states that only when all the outer pieces have been consumed can one then move on to the filets.

(You would have thought that we were a large, grabby family, but, in fact, there were just the three of us, which somehow made it worse. We perhaps had too many choices about how we would eat the pizza.)

My father takes the position that

1. he wants the filets whenever he wants them, possibly when they are hot and fresh and when he is still hungry, and that
2. he is not a signatory to any social compact.

My position is that if I eat very fast, I might consume a certain amount of pizza before the inevitable argument comes.

This never works because, after eating maybe one warm-up slice from the outer ring and thus creating the necessary channel to the filets, my father will take one of them, as if this were the most natural thing in the world, as if he were unaware that he was venturing out into disputed international filet-fishing waters, as if we were not a thoroughly crazy family.

And my mother will start a steady drumbeat of sullen protest. "Bob, you *know* you're not supposed to eat those pieces first. You're just going to make me eat the other piece faster because I'm worried. I'm going to have stomach trouble tonight because of it. What do you think you're doing?"

"What I think," my father will say, "is that people should do exactly what you tell them to do."

And we'll be off.

None of this is mischievous or playful or even the strange frictive pleasure that some long-married couples derive from getting on each other's nerves in inconsequential ways. This is bigger and meaner than that. The pizza is a Great Mandala upon which some terrible, fateful game is being played out, and its center is a collection point for the bittersweet forces surging between my parents.

Various reforms are attempted. At one point—something tells me this came after The Incident, which I am about to describe—we experiment with color-coded toothpicks. I might be green, my father blue, my mother red. (That seems symbolically about right.) In the fashion of sixteenth-century European explorers, one plants the flag of one's toothpick in a piece of pizza and claims it for future use. Only when all the pieces have been claimed by various imperialists can we begin to eat.

Actually, the flag method is a very satisfactory way of doing things, not because it is foolproof but because it makes us feel so silly that my parents are too embarrassed to fight.

No such reform is in place on the night of The Incident, in the spring of my sophomore year. The filet battle is unfolding in its usual manner, which means that I do not have a speaking role. My part involves scrunching in my seat while my colon pulses to the dull, venomous rhythm of the argument.

"Why don't you stop acting like a two-year-old?" I hear someone say. It is me. I seem to be addressing my father. My parents are both completely horrible, but my father is the aggressor and, anyway, my mother, whose indoctrination abilities would have made her a person of significant rank in the Khmer Rouge, has trained me to feel protective toward her.

"You are an ill-mannered, disgusting boor," he bellows at me.

"Don't say that," my mother tells him.

"He called me a two-year-old!"

"Well, you *are* acting like a two-year-old."

What followed exists, in my mind, only as a kind of white

light, like the flash of a nuclear blast. I had never before, during all of my childhood, directly stood up to one of my parents. It would be satisfying, sort of, to report that I now let out a flood of righteous protest, but I do not.

In fact, the "two-year-old" remark is the full measure of my rebellion. Even that is too much for the delicate balance of power in our house. We are three jiggers of nitroglycerine dangling from a Calder mobile. It takes only the trifling zephyr of my outburst to detonate us. This is not going to be like Tyler C. Tingley's outburst. It is not going to make things better.

⁂

> I have a master plan to run the world by. There are many details to be worked out—many snags to untangle. With knowing smile, you nod and cluck tongue to palate. All madmen want to run the world; few get to do so. The rest finger beads and fondle wooden dolls.
>
> *The Nemo Paradox*

What happens next? I'm honestly not sure. My recollection is that he leaves the house and doesn't come back that night and that the next place I see him is the hospital, but I suspect I may have telescoped the events to increase the sense of cause and effect and deepen my own sense of guilt.

Let us say that within a day or so, my mother comes to pick me up at school, which is unusual. It is a lovely late afternoon in the spring, redolent with the smell of cut grass and tenderly lit by the fading sun. I approach the car in a state of moderate chagrin, having just been cut from the junior varsity baseball team. After years of ineptitude in the outfield, I have been trying to adapt myself to my father's old position, first base, and a throw from second has, on this day, somehow hit me in the head. Coach Gorham Smith, who is my Latin teacher and is fond of me, has cut me to save my life, I think.

My mother tells me the news as if it were an egg whose yolk she is trying not to break. My father has been found in a motel. He is in a coma. He seems to have ingested quite a bit of alcohol and quite a few sleeping pills, although there is no way of knowing how much. There is no way of knowing anything really. There was no note.

We drive quite some distance before either of us uses any word or phrase like "suicide" or "kill himself." But eventually we do. We have no way of knowing, my mother says again, what this was. It might have been—just for example—a cry for help.

It seems like an idea for a single-panel cartoon. A woman screaming, "Help!" leans out of an upper story window of a burning building. One fireman says to another: "You never know. It might just be a cry for help."

The word "coma" turns out to be somewhat misleading. Or maybe I just have a Hollywood-tinctured notion of what a coma is: a person lying quietly. The sleeping pills my father has taken affect the central nervous system, and the overload makes him writhe and thrash in his unconscious state. His hands and feet are tied to the hospital bed, but he twists and buckles like a man wrestling a ghost. Or like Prometheus, chained to a rock and gnawed in the liver by an invisible eagle. There is a bloody bandage on his face, suggesting some kind of nasal hemorrhage. He looks wild, untamable, dangerous.

I am seized by the fear that he will wake up and try to finish the job he started. It strikes me that if he is not officially considered a suicidal patient, the hospital might not restrain or observe him.

I find a doctor and tell him my thoughts: that it is crucial my father's hands be tied, no matter what. This must sound a little strange coming from the mouth of a fifteen-year-old, but the doctor is very nice. He says he understands. My father will not be given any freedom to hurt himself until we all know what is what.

After a while, I realize I don't want to stay at the hospital. I want go to home and watch my favorite television show, which is on that night: *Ironside,* with Raymond Burr. It seems very wrong of me to want this, but I do, with a strange kind of desperation. Not even for the comforting bulk of Raymond Burr at this troubling moment but just because I want to watch the show. Because it's my favorite show and it's on, you know? How am I going to bring this up without seeming callous? I worry that if I try to watch it, my mother will rebuke me for lacking the solemnity and full focus these circumstances demand.

We do go home, and in the car, we talk over the possibility, no, the probability that this was a suicide attempt, and I tell my mother, "The only thing that makes it hard for me to believe is that I'm so important to him."

I really mean it. Even in the recent terrible times, I have never doubted my father's love. The idea that he doesn't want to be around for the rest of my youth just doesn't fit with what I know about him.

❧

I'm forty-eight now, and I want to reach into the darkness of that car, driving through Hartford on a strange night, and tell that kid he's working hard on a puzzle with three-fifths of the pieces missing. And it's not that I know now what those pieces are, only that I've arrived at a gentle agnosticism about people. We don't ever have the whole picture, and the child of the suicide is in pretty much the same boat as the biographer. People are pretty complicated, and we don't show all our cards. If you were hit by a bus tomorrow, is there a person in the world who could really explain you? Is there anyone to whom you have told your whole story, omitting nothing?

And kid, kid, kid, a person can hold two contradictory ideas in his head. A father can want to see every breath you draw *and* be off this planet, right now.

105

Colin McEnroe

𝕰𝕾

We go home. I mention, with studied casualness, that I might want to watch television, just to give my mind a break. My mother leaps at the idea with a ferocious gratitude I hadn't expected. She has been wondering what to do with me. She gets on the phone and starts calling anybody who might help her through this, which is a pretty short list because my parents have let most of their friendships lapse.

So, still feeling guilty about having trivial impulses in a momentous time, I watch Raymond Burr. I sleep. By the next morning, two uncles are on the scene. And the maroon Impala wagon has been towed from the motel where my father overdosed. He is still in a coma, and my uncles, like the rest of us, are puzzled by the lack of a note.

Yes, where is the note? How am I supposed to apply all my Beatles-tested skills to this situation with no text from which to extract clues? "She said, I know what it's like to be dead." I am trained in this stuff, but I need raw material. Where is the yellow pad?

They send me out to search the car, to make sure no such scrap has been overlooked. Or maybe to get rid of me while they discuss some horrific new aspect.

There is no note, but as I kneel in the driveway and reach under the front seat, my hand closes around something hard and smooth.

I pull a black handgun from under the seat. I think it's fair to say I have a moment of serious disorientation. Life is now a Magritte painting where objects will just kind of appear in discordant settings for no reason. "Ce n'est pas une gun." "He blew his mind out in a car. He didn't notice that the light had changed." "Happiness is a warm . . ." Bang Bang Fuck You. There are suddenly too many clues.

I walk in the house with the gun in my hand, thus provoking a startled response from the adults. And in my mother, when the significance of what I hold registers, I sense something else, almost hear her stolid Yankee fortitude snap, crumple, sag for the first time. She doesn't cry or lose her composure, but, the way a dog can sniff out your emotive states, all of us in the room sense that somehow the hull of her toughness has been breached. She is taking on water.

&

I climbed up on the end of my bunk and looked out the window. The sky is very blue, and the trees and grass are deep, rich green. I am like Lazarus. I see the world again. It is alive and extremely beautiful.

The Nemo Paradox

We get a call from the hospital. My father is conscious. When we arrive he is actually sitting up a little bit. He is, he reports, glad to be alive.

"When I woke up, I looked out the window, and the first thing I could see was that parking garage. And it was so beautiful. What a beautiful parking garage," he says.

Had he tried to kill himself?

"Oh, yes."

But he is happy he failed, he assures us again. He wants his hands untied. I don't trust him.

"It's medieval," he says, nodding his head at the restraints. Twenty-eight years later, he will use those exact words to complain about the hospital bed that hospice puts in his apartment.

We spoon-feed him some broth and Jell-O.

"How is it?" my mother asked.

"Abominable."

This is said with a trace of a smirk. He is back in his old habit of choosing words to amuse himself. It strikes me right then that he is probably telling the truth about not wanting to be dead.

Over the course of that day, he tells us a little bit more but not much. He tells us why there had been no note.

"I was trying to do a Dorothy Kilgallen," he says.

I have no idea what this means, but my mother seems to know. Dorothy Kilgallen had apparently overdosed while so inebriated that nobody could really prove it wasn't an accident. Most life insurance policies cover accidental death but not suicide, the idea being that insurance companies are offended by people having control over their own destinies. My father had hoped to leave us in a position to receive his death benefit. We don't know it then, but this is a pressing concern because he has racked up ruinous personal debts during his downward spiral.

We are broke and then some.

How about the gun?

"I had no idea what this would be like. If it were unbearably painful, I thought I would finish myself off," he says.

Jesus.

&

SADIE

What did the psychiatrist find out about your mind?

WILLIE BURKE

Nothing yet. I've only been to him seven or eight times.

SADIE

Then it's foolish. You either need an enema, a chorus girl or a ride on a roller coaster. Try all three and you'll still save money.

The Exorcism

My father is assigned to a psychiatrist who confirms that he no longer needs physical restraints. He is transferred to CCU-2, the psychiatric ward of Hartford Hospital. And there he stays for weeks. I visit every day, often taking the bus from Kingswood. My mother meets me there, and we eat dinner in the hospital cafeteria most nights. I wouldn't describe it as an idyllic time, but the sheer bulk of the hospital, populated day and night by competent, purposeful people, is comforting. We feel safe.

My father decides to tell most of his secrets to the psychiatrist and very few to us. That leaves, for him and me, a sort of Madman's Biathlon consisting of uncountable hours of ping-pong and pool in the day room. We get especially good at ping-pong with lots of lightning rallies, tickety tickety tickety, punctuated by satisfying smashes. Probably something wordless and primitive is being worked out between us in those games. As the weeks progress I begin to notice a small knot of men standing off to the side, watching, waiting for the games to be over.

These turned out to be members of a sort of cult or gang, of which my dad is the leader. They trail around after him as he agitates for various reforms, conducts his own explorations of life's mysteries, and hatches plots to confound the authorities. What are the real issues of existence, not the dopey ones they make us talk about in group? Why are we stringing beads in occupational therapy? What has that got to do with man's search for meaning? Who the hell wants ham and scalloped potatoes, mushed together in a casserole, once a week? Follow me, men. Socially awkward in most other settings, he is, in the psych ward, a kind of charismatic mountebank.

My parents decide, in their usual forthcoming fashion, to tell no one about what has happened. I am instructed not to share this story with any friends. My mother warns me—in a style now familiar to the reader—of the dire consequences should this story be widely disseminated. My father would be unemployable; we would be uninsurable; we would all die in the streets.

It would be necessary to say something to the world.

"I have been thinking about that," my father says on the first or second day after his awakening, "and it struck me that 'nervous breakdown' might be the best we could do." My mother vetoes it. She isn't having any truck with nervous breakdowns. The official explanation is that my father accidentally took "a toxic combination of medications." I say the words "toxic combination of medications" so many times in so many situations that it acquires the numbing meter of a litany. Another goddamned secret.

My mother has a high-pressure, low-paying job as an office manager in an industry-lobbying firm. Every day, she holds that together without cracking, but at night, the anxieties overwhelm her. She cannot fall asleep unless I lie in my father's twin bed. Welcome to Thebes-on-the-Connecticut. It's sort of Oedipus Lite. I have almost killed Dad and am almost sleeping with Mom.

And then one day he comes home. My mother and I are uneasy. We have come to find the whole nuthouse sky rather sheltering. Everything is so secure and professional over there in the hospital. Werner's house seems, by contrast, infested with land mines and staffed by amateurs.

But my father really is better. This is not a course of therapy I would recommend to most people, but in his unique circumstances, a self-induced near-death experience was just the ticket. He is happier than I've ever seen him, and his old gentleness, familiar from my childhood, has returned. It is nearly impossible to talk about my father without resorting to polytheistic imagery, with his gnomes and fairies and incubi and little people. So let me say that all that booze and Seconal appears to have flushed the demons out of him.

"It sounds crazy," he writes to me, years and years later, "but the act of suicide is a positive act and not a negative one.

The suicider revs himself up and does the deed he feels must be done . . . Suicide is not a passive act. The man who puts his head in an oven or points a gun at his head may appear to be gently giving up the ghost. This is not true. It takes a great deal of emotional effort—misguided or not—to take one's life."

⁂

What is alarming is how much of this is predicted in his play *The Exorcism.*

Here is Willie, discussing his possession with the priest, Father Reagan:

FATHER REAGAN
Your soul is in danger. Your soul is in grave danger.

WILLIE BURKE
Will there be prayers and incantations?

REAGAN
Yes.

WILLIE
Will there be admonitions to the devil?

REAGAN
Yes.

WILLIE
Will there be a struggle between the forces of good and evil?

REAGAN
Yes.

WILLIE
A mighty struggle?

REAGAN

Enough of a struggle to get the job done.

WILLIE

Will legions of angels be employed?

REAGAN

Unfortunately, the chancery can't command such
forces—or perhaps it can—who knows? Who knows
what forms help from heaven takes?

WILLIE

Then there will be a battle and I will have an
observation post on the front lines.

REAGAN

You will be the front lines.

WILLIE

I will be an Agincourt, a Hastings, a Verdun, a
Bastogne, a field of white lilies for demons to
bleed upon. I shall know the sound of heaven's
fury. I shall smell the burning brimstone and
hear the screams of creatures hell cannot torment. Then the forces of evil will fall back in
disorder, snarling, belching fire and sulphur.
It will become a rout, with angels in hot pursuit of screaming imps. At the last there will
be calm. There will be peace. There will be
flowers everywhere and the soft vibrations of a
million violins. Into this calm, beauty and
serenity will come a voice—a soft voice, a
soothing voice. The voice will say, "You're better now, Willie." And I will nod without speaking, for it is the fate of battlefields to offer
mute testimony of the futility of war.

It is difficult to tell whether Willie is gravely serious or amusing himself at the priest's expense. And of course, it is a mistake, in treating of Irishmen, to assume there is any distinction. What is clear to me is that my father describes, with prescience and precision, the experience he will have three years later.

The play is also quite clear about who the enemy is, about whom Willie truly must vanquish. (We'll come to that. I promise.)

He tried writing the story of his demons.

That didn't work.

He had to do it. He had to make himself the battlefield.

"The person prone to suicide carries a rage within—a rage to kill," he writes to me in that letter, years later. "He wants to kill because he cannot endure himself . . . He hates himself. Because he hates himself, he cannot relate to others. Nothing is gained by showing him somebody who is worse off than he. He can't relate to the difference."

❧

They send me back upstairs to Colinworld, with instructions to do my homework. I have been keeping up and make high honors at the end of the semester. My father sits me down after and thanks me in a "You are to be commended for maintaining your sterling academic performance even during a period when I tried to kill myself" speech that I bet not a lot of parents give.

It strikes me that I have my parents over a barrel for once. If I want to become a juvenile delinquent now, who is in a position to remonstrate with me? My father tried to kill himself! I can shoot up on public buses, and nobody can really fault me. But I do not avail myself. I take no drugs or chances or liberties.

One afternoon in late May, my father picks me up at Kingswood. We walk through the gates to where his fateful

Impala—you wanna talk about a car named Angst—is parked on Outlook Avenue. There is an ambulance idling by the side of the road, its driver slumped back in the front seat, his elbow hanging out of the open window. He turns his head toward us and calls to my father by name.

It is Norman Cristina, our ex-neighbor and disgraced firefighter, reborn as an ambulance driver—a rather terrifying thought. In fact, a month or two later, he is in the paper again, this time for delivering a baby in his ambulance. "I bet he pulled over and waited for the little bastard to come out," my father says delightedly when he reads it.

This time, though, Norman asks if he can have a word with my father in private. I step away and they speak briefly. My father walks back to his car laughing and wagging his head. He tells me what was said.

"The last time I saw you, you didn't look so good," Norman told him.

In an odds-shattering twist, Norman was the ambulance driver who arrived on the scene of my father's suicide attempt.

"When I saw it was you, I really stepped on the gas," Norman said.

Considering Norman's penchant for heroism, my father muses, "I was probably in a hell of a lot more danger from crashing in the goddamned ambulance."

And he laughs until his shoulders shake.

❧

The next fall, I, a lifelong boy, become an Oxford girl. And our household welcomes a new arrival in the person of Henry Nemo. Why does this sound like a sitcom installment?

Kingswood, a boys' school, and Oxford, a girls' school, have done the paperwork necessary to merge the two institutions, but the sticky feat of getting boys and girls to sit side-by-side in classrooms has yet to be accomplished.

The campuses are about three miles apart. In this, my junior year, the planners begin stirring small amounts of us into one another. A handful of classes are set up as evenly mixed boy-girl blends, and a shuttle bus runs between the two places. The driver is Charlie, a pudgy and lecherous man who entertains us—when only boys are on the bus—with filthy talk. He is our Charon—the figure in Greek mythology who poled the ferryboat across the river Styx to the world of the dead—but our passage is from the safe, arid, monastic world of a boys' school to the damp, viscous caverns of Oxford.

In that handful of mixed classes is my fourth-year Latin class with Mr. O'Brien. So few people have stuck with Latin that, in order to have a respectable quorum ("of whom," genitive plural, right Obie?), it is necessary to combine the boys and girls classes and throw in the one and only guy who is taking third-year Latin.

We read the *Aeneid*. If you are already feeling a little protective of your father, the *Aeneid* is a damn strange thing to read, because it is nearly obsessed with "paternitas," the Roman ideal of fatherhood. The epic's most memorable image is probably that of Aeneas bearing his father Anchises on his back from the burning ruins of Troy.

I am also trying to study French and am required to take American history, and it is all kind of impossible to schedule, unless . . . unless . . . Would I be willing to spend most of my day over at Oxford, taking American history and French courses in which I would be the only boy?

I am weeks shy of sixteen. I have a hard time, in these days, imagining problems for myself. After what I have been through recently, what could be so bad?

"I'll do it."

❧

Word gets around to my peers. There are raucous expressions of envy. What a deal! Be like shooting fish in a barrel.

Oh, yes, I say with a weak grin, shooting fish in a barrel.

Inside, I am already beginning to wonder about those fish, that barrel.

I am a slightly lonely, awkward person. I have been attending a school where almost everybody else has more money and better clothes. I am commissioner, and, for that matter, Yahweh, of an imaginary basketball league. My father communes with fairies. I am entering my fifth year at a boys' school. I know more about certain microorganisms than I know about girls.

Worse still, I look absolutely horrible.

Hormones have been working me over, jabbing me with a stick.

I am skinny and pimply. My hair is ill-shorn, and my clothes never seem to fit right. The effort of keeping all my secrets and maintaining the requisite sangfroid and cynical detachment in a school full of would-be Holden Caufields has done something even worse to my face than the ravages of acne. My visage is crimped and tight and unsmiling.

In the recipe for romantic success, I seem an unlikely ingredient.

⁓❧

Stirring in my father's mind is the character of Henry Nemo, a writer convicted of terrible crimes against women. Emerging from a four-year fugue state into a howling, violent rage, Nemo is given a lobotomy. ("They bored two 1¼-inch holes in my skull so that they could get at the underside of the frontal lobe. The cutting was orbital—whatever that means.")

My father is back at the business of staying up late, flashing black lightning down on his yellow pads, but this time it is a novel, his first.

It is my idea.

"Why don't you write something about what it was like to

wake up surprised that you were still alive?" I tell him. "Make it a novel. You're getting nowhere with plays."

I am actually beginning to suspect he doesn't like plays. He hasn't seen one—written by himself or anybody else—in years.

I also donate the name, explaining that Nemo is Greek for "nobody." I touch upon the confusion this causes between Odysseus and the Cyclops.

⁊♣

Nemo awakens from his lobotomy and cannot recall his own name or any details of his past. He is terrified. A note on his chart reports, "Patient told maintenance man that God didn't know what he was doing. God very inefficient, confused. Job too big for God."

After several days of recovery, locked in a cell, Nemo is allowed to use the washroom.

In his makeshift journal, he writes, "I couldn't bring myself to write down what I saw. What I saw was me. I don't know what the hell I expected—some sort of happy-go-lucky guy with a decent, well-meaning face, friendly and open with a warm smile and twinkling eye. Forget it. Let's not talk about it. We'll talk about something else. *I'm ugly!* I'm the ugliest-looking man on earth! I jumped when I saw myself in the mirror. I wiped the mirror over and over with my towel. I thought it was coated with something. It wasn't. As I shaved, I kept hoping it would get better. It didn't. I have a Neanderthal brow. My eyes are hard and mean-looking. My nose has been broken. Somebody or something bit a piece off one of my ears. I seem to have most of my teeth, but when I smile, it's like a shark biting on an oil drum. From the neck down I'm quite impressive. My thing caused quite a bit of comment in the shower room, but the face is what the world looks at. I don't want the world staring at my face. What woman would let me come near her?"

This is—except for the thing part—roughly how I feel

about how I look. At a boys' school, it hasn't mattered much to me. Suddenly it does. I don't want to be Henry Nemo at Oxford.

I have a plan for survival among those Amazons. My plan is to be smart and possibly also funny. I am afraid of women. In my life thus far I have dated one girl, briefly and uneventfully. She ended things, hoping (in vain) to trade up to my friend Mark Fisher, who had spent the entire decade, ever since we met in first grade, being more handsome and popular than me.

No more heartbreak. These Oxford girls might not like me much, I reason, but I will see to it that they respect me.

I am a peculiar boy.

❧

So I study. For my French course, taught by a Miss French, I simply do my homework, pause, and do it all over again. I am flawless every day.

American history is more problematic. The teacher, Miss Hall, is in her final year before retirement. She regards my arrival in the last gasp of her 137-year boy-free teaching career as some kind of cruel joke. The girls are seniors, a year older than me. It will be necessary, I reason, to read two texts: the one that is assigned and another, more detailed and challenging book I find in my father's detailed and challenging library. The result is that I am always grotesquely over-prepared for class and eager to undertake issues that do not at all conform to Miss Hall's understanding of American history.

To worsen matters, I am shipwrecked at Oxford for most of the day with nothing to do and no mates around. So I re-read everything.

I am afraid to go to lunch because I think no one will want to eat with me. So I don't eat lunch. I lose exorbitant amounts of weight.

In time, I become the world's foremost six-foot-tall, 128-pound French-speaking American-history expert.

My aspect is that of a sullen, distempered caged animal. Much later, Oxford girls will tell me they were troubled in those days by the way I kept my head down and never smiled. They wondered why I didn't eat.

Despite the fact that I am insufferably competent and never attempt to return anyone's friendship, some girls try to be kind. One of them, a girl named Sue, simply insists that I talk to her. I have found a place where I can be alone between periods. It is the lobby looking out on Highland Street, with a view of the nursing home where, twenty-seven years later, my father will die.

I like to sit in a Windsor chair, tilting it back so it rocks and bumps gently against the wall while I *bump-bump* mentally palpate, say, the legacy *bump-bump* of James K. Polk. Sometimes the teacher on the other side of the wall, Mrs. Gettier, emerges and, in exasperation, implores me to stop. One last, soothing pleasure halted, I think. Sue comes to the lobby each day, sits down in another chair, and makes conversation until, falteringly, I join in. There is nothing romantic in her overtures. She has a nice boyfriend, I know. She is just being decent to me.

And I am wildly in love with her for it. Like the Beast, like Quasimodo, like the Phantom, I am hideous but I can be reached.

I love them all, actually. In their dreadful gray uniforms, every single one of them is pretty to me, in various ways. And I yearn for them and dream of romances and, by remaining pathologically aloof, make absolutely certain that none of them suspects that one as ugly and wretched as I entertain such dreams.

❧

"Women, children, and dogs over seven pounds know all about love, but men only experience it in their teens and twenties when the temperature is over sixty-five," Henry Nemo observes as my father pours him out onto yellow pads at our dining room table. I have moved down from Colinworld and now we work together most nights, with me advising him on the novel.

I am uniquely connected to the Nemo material because at school I continue to feel like a loveless, isolated freak.

One day, while I work in the library, a Swedish exchange student, a pretty girl from my history class, comes to me to ask about a word, in English, whose meaning she cannot divine. She writes it on my notebook.

"Bliss."

She looks at me inquiringly.

"Happiness. Great joy," I whisper hoarsely.

Bliss. I'm a real expert.

Another day, in the spring, two mischievous girls plunk themselves down in my lobby and discuss, a little too audibly, their menstrual cycles.

The lobby is never quite the same after that.

There is also a smell, sweet and rank, I encounter when entering a classroom that has been closed for a while. It's a dense smell of perfume inexpertly applied and experimental hair products and something else, something pent up and hormonal. I believe it is the smell of fresh, excited, wonderful girls cooped up all day without boys.

It makes me think I am not alone in my yearnings.

❧

In mythology, Aeneas founds Rome. Before he does that, he visits the underworld, where the shades of the dead dwell. In *The Hero with a Thousand Faces,* the scholar Joseph Campbell says those two things are closely related. He writes that in all sorts of legends "the really creative acts are represented as those deriving from some sort of dying to the world." The hero disappears and then returns, licked and seared by infernal flames, filled with new energy. Think of Luke Skywalker when he comes to retrieve Han Solo at the start of *Return of the Jedi*. His hand has been chopped off, and Mark Hamill, the actor who plays him, has almost obligingly damaged his real face in a motorcycle accident. Our first look into his eyes tells us the boyish Luke has died away. This new person is someone who has marched back from the world of the dead and is one hell of a lot more powerful and dangerous.

To grow, to become formidable, one must die.

This is the lesson of 1970.

The school year passes. Pius Aeneas gets in and out of scrapes. Manifest Destiny comes and goes. I am frequently out sick for long stretches thanks to my rigorous nutrition program. The effort of looking serious and unapproachable all day gives my face an additionally sour cast. I am increasingly nobody's prize.

The word "bliss," etched on my notebook in Swedish ballpoint, mocks my progress through life.

And then spring comes. The temperature is over sixty-five.

Spring has always been good to me. I thaw, in various ways. In this case, my pimple count decreases. I am named editor of the school newspaper. It seems possible, maybe permissible, to return the occasional smile at Oxford. At home, I am Aeneas, carrying my father on my shoulders out of the burning ruins of our recent past. Or so I imagine.

I do not see that he is Aeneas. He is the one who has visited the eerie underworld of the dead, perhaps even communed with the shade of his own father. His psychiatrist is telling him he is at last free, filled with creative power. There will be a new empire of plays and novels, streaming from his fingers like light from the godhead. This is not, alas, an accurate prophecy, but it is true that his time in the Bardo, the waiting room between death and rebirth, has made him wiser and stronger.

I remember one of the last days of that year. It is bright and sunny. I put down my book in the lobby, walk outside, and lie down on a low wall, letting the sun get at my acne.

It feels good.

A girl walks out of the main building. She lies down near me and takes the sun. We say very little, and I don't see her again for twenty-seven years.*

Her name is Joy.

Great joy.

❧

I spend the summer alone in thought for long stretches of each day, stalled in a Court of Pizza Pie Powder. After a series of continuances, the Court drops its case against me.

When I return to school, Tyler C. Tingley sits me down.

"Your skin has cleared up," he says.

"Yes."

He looks at me, as if he is trying to guess what has been wrong with me for two years. I still have not told anyone the suicide story.

"You're going to be fine," he says, finally.

---

*Life often seems to loop back on itself in strange ways. Think of Norman Cristina, who entered our story as a firebug and departed as my father's rescuer. The next time I see Joy, twenty-seven years have passed. She is head of the hospice program caring for my father in the last weeks of his life.

Four

MOST HaPPy FIMLY

Sarah Whitman Hooker Pies recommended with this chapter

- ◆ Uncle John's Gentle Fig Apricot Fluff
- ◆ Wolfpack Jack Tarpaper Crust over Nutcracker Peach Pit Pie
- ◆ Mango Mango Bang

❧

On October 6, 1954, my father answers a letter from a man compiling an encyclopedia of the theater:

> I learned playwriting by writing plays in my spare time while working at a factory in East Hartford, Connecticut. I wrote eleven plays before having one optioned. The eleventh play, *Mulligan's Snug*, was optioned by eight producers and rewritten twenty-three times, but never produced. The

twelfth play, *The Silver Whistle,* was produced by the Theatre Guild. The thirteenth play, *Summer Motley,* was optioned once. The fourteenth play, *The Distaff Paradox,* was optioned twice. I am working on the fifteenth.

I was born in New Britain, Connecticut, July 1, 1916, and attended the University of Chicago. I have no degrees, never studied dramatics, and know little or nothing about the theater. I have forgotten why I started writing plays. In spite of the fact that I have had a play on Broadway, I am convinced that I would be better off today had I invested my time more wisely. I have taken three different batteries of vocational tests which showed that I have no talent as a writer. In other words, being a playwright doesn't make sense, but I have too much time invested to back out now.

❧

The following day, October 7, 1954, a car rolls down Chestnut Hill in Glastonbury. It's late afternoon, and the people in the car enjoy the reddening light as it falls on the trees and fields that line the steeply sloping road.

The car turns right on Main Street and drives briskly toward the center of town. Glastonbury is mainly, in '54, a sleepy town of woods, meadows, brooks, and farms. Dairy farmers grow tons of silage down along the Connecticut River and truck it to their herds, a little ways upland.

The car pulls into the small business district. The people get out and do some errands. Then, ready to leave, they back their enormous Oldsmobile out and begin to drive away. There comes a squeal of tires, the splintering smash of metal and glass. Another car has hit the Olds, and the two cars now sit pinned to each other, their shapes distorted into Louise Nevelson abstractions. The clap of metal brings people running from all directions. The driver of the other car gets out. He watches as the two people climb out of the Olds, and then he begins to quake. The people rushing to the scene see the same thing and shout excitedly.

The woman getting out of the passenger's side is nine months pregnant.

The woman is thirty-two, New England pretty, brunette, soft cheeks, delicate nose.

This is 1954, and a white, well-dressed pregnant woman is a cultural divinity, the perfect symbol for America's postwar self-exaltation. A pregnant woman climbing out of a smoking heap of battered aluminum is a shard snapped off a poisonous national nightmare.

The man who hit the Olds is apologizing frantically, and the people on the scene are offering help of all kinds and battering her with questions. All of the sound compresses to a thin wire of wordless anxiety strung across her mind. She runs her hand across her ridiculous ball of a stomach. What has happened?

The woman is my mother. My father is driving the Olds.

That's me in there.

We're fine.

Nobody knows that, not even the doctor.

"The birth may come tonight," he says. "We'll be prepared for your call."

There is no call. I am not born. After a few days, everybody calms down and waits through the final week.

My mother feels the first twinge of real contractions on a morning in October. Clouds and winds are swirling in from the ocean, and the radio bleats out suggestions of a hurricane. All through the day the storm builds, and my parents feel their own pulses joined to its surges. In the early afternoon, they leave the house on Chestnut Hill and drive to the hospital through a curtain of whirling leaves as tree limbs snap and saplings topple.

They wait there for ten hours, and then I am born in the night, at 11:29 P.M. My mother is thirty-two, and my father is thirty-eight. I am their first child, the only one they will have.

They are old to be first-time parents in the Eisenhower Era. They have lived for short spells on Fifth Avenue and in Beverly Hills. Nowhere feels right to my father, and now the money is running a little lower. They are living in a rented house out in the country, and that doesn't feel right either.

ঌ৪

He doesn't want a child. He doesn't think of families in a very happy way. He says no, again and again. It will be horrible. It will disrupt his life. My mother begins to think she might leave him.

When I am born, he walks down to the hospital nursery to observe me.

He goes back to my mother's room.

"Well?" asks my mother.

"What?"

"How does he look?"

"He doesn't look so good," my father says.

"What?"

"He doesn't look so good."

"What's wrong with him?"

"He's a baby. You know how babies look."

"How do they look?"

"Babies never look so good."

"Go and look again."

He departs. He returns.

"He looks like a tiger."

"What does *that* mean?"

"You know how tigers look."

He calls me "Tiger" for the rest of my childhood. I don't hear him say "Colin" until my voice changes.

Happy? He goes nuts.

He is up for the 3 A.M. feeding. He's at the side of my crib the second I wake up, eager to start the day with me. What's the big deal with elves when you have a real live little person all your own? This, too, lasts for most of my childhood. He never turns me down. Play catch? Board game? Read the funnies? Go for a ride? Pick up hamburgers and bring them home, dripping juice into their wax paper? Throw a football? Go to the zoo? The answer is almost never no.

❧

Because of *Mulligan's Snug*, he is hired in 1959 to write the book for a Broadway musical version of *The Quiet Man*, a Maurice Walsh short story that has also been turned into a 1952 movie starring John Wayne. It is the story of an American prizefighter who tries to retire to Ireland after accidentally killing a man in the ring. Having vowed to himself never to fight again, he falls in love with a woman who, for complicated reasons, will not be released into wedlock until he fights her brother.

For a couple of years my dad is gone a lot, first on trips to New York and then for the out-of-town runs in Philadelphia and Washington, D.C. And then back to New York for the Broadway opening. The play is called *Donnybrook!* Its stars include Art Lund and Susan Johnson, both formerly of *Most Happy Fella*.

I am in first grade.

Broadway is a tough thing for me to grasp. He goes away. I miss him. He comes back, usually with a great toy. Small plastic men are my favorite things, and once he brings a box of knights with moveable limbs and swords and lances that can be fitted into their hands. For all of my childhood tiny plastic men will be my toys of choice, men who can be set up and assigned identities, who can be walked and flown through various conflicts and dramas. Hours and hours on the floor with men. They are the toys, I suppose, of a slightly lonely boy, but also of a boy who feels the invisible presence of tiny people.

My mother and I drive to New York City to watch a dress rehearsal. It is the practice in those days to hold dress rehearsals in the Bowery, which is a very bad place in 1961, populated by bums, in the parlance of the times. A child of the Connecticut suburbs, I have never seen bums.

Once inside the theater, I watch very carefully and comprehend maybe one-tenth of the plot. I am aware that one of the men onstage is very funny, and my eyes are drawn to him. He wears a derby and a ratty suit. Every twitch of his face, every bowing of his small, rubbery body seems to get a laugh. I can't stop watching him. He is Eddie Foy Jr., a vaudevillean since the age of seven who has starred in other Broadway hits, notably *The Pajama Game*.

I don't know anything about that.

I just want to be that man, get those laughs.

After the show, we go back out to the car. The bums are standing around it. One of them is urinating on the car. We go back into the theater for help. I'm a little scared.

"Who are those men?"

"They're bums," my mother says. "They don't have any money. They don't have any jobs."

"How does that happen?"

"It could happen to you if you don't watch out."

Wrong thing to say to me.

For weeks I worry about becoming a bum. I lie in bed and close my eyes, and there I am, in my rags, stinking and stumbling through the Bowery.

I am too young to be included on Broadway opening night, but even back home in West Hartford I am a minor celebrity. The reviews are mixed, mostly good, even some raves. Our first grade class is ordered by the teacher to write letters of congratulation to the playwright.

From Christine Laski:

Dear Mr. McEnroe
you are Writing a good play. your work in a Room. I bet your work

is heard is it. I bet colin likes you very much! Are your fimly HaPPy. They are very HaPPy. Who are the people in the play?

I go back to New York to see the play staged at the 46th Street Theater. I hang around for the weekend, seeing the show twice, finding myself ushered into Eddie Foy's dressing room for several audiences. He likes me.

"Get him in the front row, stage left," he instructs my father. "Then when I fall down at the end of 'Wisha-Wurra,' I'll take off my hat and put it on his head."

Oh, please? I'm going to get one of Eddie Foy's laughs.

I am sent back home before this can happen.

Back in Miss Barasso's first grade class, it is show-and-tell.

I have now seen *Donnybrook!* three times. Would anyone like to hear a song from the show?

Why, yes!

What I have in mind is one of Foy's big numbers, a duet with Susan Johnson called "I Wouldn't Bet One Penny." I'm going to get some of Eddie Foy's applause if it kills me.

It begins innocently enough,

You could never tempt me with insinuatin' queries
Asking me to come have tea,
But suppose you picked a rainy afternoon,
Well, ma'am
Strong as I am,
I wouldn't bet one penny on the way I'd be.

So far, so good.

But it has not occurred to me that the standards and practices of the Broadway stage might be slightly more adventurous than those of Miss Barasso's first grade class in 1961.

So that when I sing

I support my standards with a will that never wearies
Think of what you tried on me
But if you saved one trick that made the others swoon
Oh, well . . .
Damn it to hell.
I wouldn't bet one penny on the . . .

I am startled to see Miss Barasso leap out of her seat and order me down to the principal's office.

Dr. Martin, a woman, has a dark and quiet office. She herself is a small, dark, and quiet woman. She peers at me through the gloom.

"Now. I understand you've caused a stir."

"I was just singing a song! It's in my father's play."

"Tell me about this play."

I sketch out the opening scene and sing a few bars of "Sez I," the first number.

"More."

I sing the second number, "The Day the Snow Is Melting."

"What happens next?"

I am gone from my classroom for more than an hour. By the time I return, most of the students assume I have been expelled and, possibly, beheaded. Even Miss Barasso has a wondering stare.

Dr. Martin calls my mother.

"You have a remarkable boy."

"We think so, too."

"He has just been in my office."

"Oh, dear."

"He performed every song in *Donnybrook!* And quite a lot of the dialogue."

"Oh, my."

"You have a remarkable boy."

My father is still in New York. My mother calls him with the story. He passes it along to Eddie Foy, complete with the "Damn it to hell" in class.

"Bring him back to New York," Foy exclaims. "I'll take him out on the town. I'll buy him any toy he wants in FAO Schwarz."

Somehow, this never happens either. But every night for weeks, I fall asleep nursing a vision more sugary than my life as a bum. Eddie Foy and I are in FAO Schwarz. I am pointing to a stuffed animal, a rabbit as big as a horse.

ॐ

In second grade, there is no play. *Donnybrook!* closes after sixty-five performances. I have to find another way to be remarkable.

"You're a midget." This is my mother talking.

"What's a midget?"

"Somebody who never gets tall."

"I'm never going to get tall?"

"No. You'll always be this size. You're fifteen years old."

"We held you out of school for a while," my father chimes in absentmindedly.

I fall silent, playing with my tiny plastic men.

And then, "I'm really fifteen?"

"Yes."

I spend the weekend as a midget.

On Monday, at school, I tell my friends. It seems to me I'm entitled to a certain respect.

"I'm fifteen."

"You are not."

"I'm a midget."

"What's that?"

I explain.

"Miss Clarke! Colin says he's fifteen. He says he's a midget."

"I'm sure he's not."

"I am! My parents said so!"

"I'm sure you misunderstood."

It takes a week or two to get this straightened out. I suffer a tremendous loss of face when it comes out that I am normal. I get mad at my parents, not for convincing me I was a midget but for subsequently breaking cover. It seems to me we all should have stuck to our story.

☙

The first time anybody in our household ever dies, it is me. "Crawford? Sam?"

I know what I am doing on the eastern edge of Mooney's Woods on a winter afternoon in West Hartford, 1963. I am looking for two friends I think might be there.

"Crawford? Sam?"

I am eight years old.

What I don't know is why I walk out on the ice of the pond that lies down the hill, out of sight, behind the Simmons house on Staples Place. The ice is perfect for skateless sliding—one, two, three, glide. I have been told to stay off the ice. One, two, three, glide. "Crawford? Sam?"

The ice abruptly gives way beneath my feet and I drop straight down into the cold water of the pond. No one can see me. No one can possibly hear my cry for help.

My boots fill with water. They are those black boots of yore, with the agreeable buckles whose little hinged tongues slipped through little metal grillworks. They battened so nicely onto your leg that you could not possibly kick them off.

I sit here now watching my young self sink and kick, and it strikes me that every requisite of sudden, untimely death is in place. I am alone, sinking through icy water in a secluded pond. I am the only person who can save me, and I am not strong or athletic.

I survive mainly because the bulky, ungainly coat I am wearing spreads out over the water in a way that traps a big bubble of air. If I were an angel worshipper, I suppose I could make this into an angel, but it is more like a big bubble of air. It keeps me high in the water and upright while I clamber up on the ice—only to have more of it break away.

How do I get myself out? I can't remember. I just do.

My next decision almost kills me. For some reason, I walk home, a distance of several blocks. I pass at least one other person on the trip and sob out to him what has happened to me, but it doesn't occur to me to go to a warm house right away.

My father hears an odd noise coming from outdoors and concludes it is an animal in distress. It is my wail of misery, fright, danger, and near-death.

By the time I barge through the door of our apartment, ice has formed all over me. It hangs off my coat in jagged formations. I present myself to my father who, years later, will admit to being completely terrified. At this moment, he seems merely businesslike about getting me into a bath and gradually warming the water. That a person from Miami Beach knows to do this is one of life's little blessings.

That night my parents stay up late. It will seem to them, years later, that the news that night carries other stories of boys who fell through the ice, and that those boys died. I doubt it. I think that for days and weeks and maybe even years, every story of a boy who falls through the ice and dies becomes another inflection of me, an alternative form of their son whose luck, this time, runs out.

My father's memory will be that, after his ministerings that day, my vitality is restored. In his story, he is Christ, and I am Lazarus. In truth, I am not so easily fixed.

Within days, I have pneumonia. I recover. The pneumonia comes back. I recover again. At least, I think so. The act of writing this has made me feel cold, has turned an awl of pain loose in my chest. I can see the bony fingers of the trees and a gray-white sky of that day.

My father, well into my adult life, will give me a series of winter coats as Christmas presents. They are invariably the gray-beige colorless color of the coat that saved me. Coat after coat, never with any particular comment.

Life renders us. This is no secret. It boils away layers each day. Every so often, I am convinced, life conspires to kill off characters inside us. The unremarkable boy of that day, not especially good at being himself, dies in the pond, and someone a little bit different grows into his skin.

≈❧

In third grade, there is a career pageant.

We are instructed to compose a couplet describing our future job. We must go up on stage with a prop or two and recite the couplet.

God help me, I am up there with a toy typewriter.

Some folks would rather be a wrestler or a fighter,
but I would like to be a writer.

When my father is not writing he shows houses. It takes him away from me on weekends a lot, because that's when people like to look at houses. Sometimes I tag along, and my childhood memories are splashed with the rattle of "For Sale" signs in the backs of station wagons and the aroma of freshly hewn wood in the brand-new houses and the echoing clap of men's shoes on bare wood floors.

"I have to show three houses today." Even then it sounds like an odd phrasing. I have to show you a place in the woods where diamond-shaped orange mushrooms grow. I have to show you how to throw a curve ball. I have to show you the place where I was born. But houses are so big and obvious. They need to be shown?

Missing is any mention of the people. My father always has

to "show houses" but rarely to anyone. He doesn't mention clients or customers because he is so hilariously a parody of the paradigmatic American Salesman circa 1962: good with eye contact, with names, with light chatter. My father is an introvert's introvert. He prefers looking down or off into fairyland. He can't remember the names, even, of his co-workers or our household pets. A cat of ours, Mackenzie, is still, after ten years, "the gray-and-white cat."

When he pictures "people" in his mind, he pictures two-legged beings who bray out perfectly human—and therefore grotesquely irrational—responses to houses. They fixate on some quirk of a house's appearance. The carpet, the kitchen floor, the wallpaper throw them for a loop. They cannot be lured down into the basement.

"The basement of a house tells its story," my father explains. Water, strange fuse boxes, makeshift reinforcements to ancient joists, termites. These are the things you must behold. Once, he and I see a septic system out-pipe with a high-tech warning device on it, suggesting some imminent Chernobyl of poop.

"People don't want to look at things like that in the basement," he grumbles. "They want to look at the goddamned mullioned windows."

For the right client, though, he is a godsend.

"We'd be pulling up to a house, and as we were slowing down, before the car even came to rest at the curb, I would say, 'No,' and he'd just put his foot back on the gas and begin pulling away, not a word from him," says a woman who bought two houses from him. She cackles at the memory. "Any other agent would have tried to make me go in, see all the great features that weren't apparent on the outside, all that crap. He just drove us away. I *loved that!*"

"How come you never take me to church?"

"We don't go to church."

"Other kids, their parents take them to church."

"You want us to take you to church?"

"Yeah!"

So they do. It turns out that they mean "take you to church" rather literally. They drive up to the church. The car disgorges me. They drive home to smoke Fatimas and read the papers. They come back and retrieve me when it's over.

They pick my denominations, although I am never sure on what basis. For starters, I am a Presbyterian, but later I will transfer to Universalism, get traded to the Episcopalians, and finish out my career, like Willie Mays on the Mets, as a Congregationalist.

They attend none of these churches. I am a latchkey Protestant.

This arrangement has enormous appeal to Bob McEnroe. Having enthusiastically repudiated his native Catholicism, he now has new worlds to conquer. He can be a heretic, an apostate, in several other sects. Each time I move to a new church, he reads up on its denominational theology. Then he shows up a couple of times a year and argues with the minister. Universalism, for some reason, is his favorite. The Universalist books pile up around his chair. He takes copious notes. William Ellery Channing should know so much about Universalism. The minister, a sweet-tempered old guy named Fiske, poor bastard, learns to fear the sight of my father coming up over the horizon at coffee hour, flying the Jolly Roger, ready to engage him on hairsplitting points of antitrinitarianism.

In seventh grade, there is an Easter pageant at the Universalist church, and I am Jesus. It is a speaking role. Cosmologically, nothing could be more second rate than to be a Universalist Jesus. It's like being Nepal's greatest basketball star.

No one cares. You're not divine. You don't get the girls that the Methodist Jesuses get.

I believe my main job that day is to handle the "woman at the well" situation. I show up with my game face on. I am fully backgrounded. I spend the preceding Saturday night memorizing Jesus' lines. I tell everybody what is what, as only Jesus can.

My father, sitting in an audience of fifty, is, by all evidence, enthralled. My later acting stints, in front of much larger high school audiences and working with slightly more challenging material and benefiting from better production values, will fail to impress him at all.

On this day, however, for reasons I cannot fathom, I have him in the palm of my hand. He will tell people, for the rest of his life, what a great Universalist Jesus I was. He will bring it up with me a couple of times a year, for the next thirty-two years.

"You know, you were a great Jesus that time."

"Yes, you've mentioned. Has anything else I have done ever impressed you?"

"You just had everything under control that day."

Is he putting me on? I have no idea.

He's not always easy to read on this God stuff. When I am five, he overhears my friend Ruthie Saphirstein tell me there is no Santa Claus. He tells her—in a spirit of genial nihilism—that Moses was a fake. This is a joke, but it takes quite a bit of smoothing over by my mother with the Jewish families in our apartment complex.

❧

Is our fimly HaPPy? I bet this work is h(e)ard, is it?

It is. It's very h(e)ard.

So h(e)ard, in fact, that we are not getting anywhere with anything. Boy, does he ever have a lot of time to spend with me. Play catch? Go to the zoo? Bronx Zoo has Komodo dragons. Take a drive down there? See the dragons?

He is still funny. He is still in touch with little people.

At the real estate office, each phone has a row of buttons that light up in sequence as the lines are engaged. When the last button lights up out of sequence, he has divined, it always means that someone has tried to call the Harte Volkswagen dealership and has misdialed.

Once he figures this out, he makes a point of being the one to answer those calls.

"Ja?" he begins. And then, in a dreadful German accent, "Dis is der Black Forest Volksvagen Company."

"Oh. I'm not sure I have the right number. Is this . . ."

"Ja!" And then he goes on at some length about the elves in the Black Forest, who make the Volkswagen parts with great care and pride in their magic.

Then he tries to sell the hapless caller a Volkswagen kit for $750. He dilates upon the money-saving advantages, the easy-to-read instructions, his willingness to lend the proper tools, and, of course, the everlasting gratitude of the elves.

He never sells even one kit because, near the end of his spiel, he reveals that the instructions, although easy to read, are in German. I suspect he occasionally crosses a line and begins to believe there really is a kit for him to sell. Boundaries are never his strong point.

෨ඊ

Fourth grade. It is teacher conference day. I am home alone. Outside, the rain pours, cold and pitiless. The day hums with bad portent.

My mother steps through the back door. She is a swarm of wet bees. She is a demon hissing steam.

She shows me the report card. Many Cs. She shows me where a D—a D!—in penmanship has been changed to a C, with the teacher scrubbing off the epidermis of the paper to get rid of the letter written in ballpoint. The C is muddily inscribed on the

paper's festering wound. The grade change has not been occa-
sioned by a reappraisal of my penmanship but by her bullying of
the teacher. I have, in fact, D penmanship, but no child of hers
is going to get a D. She says so. She will later find out that
Norman Mailer's mother did exactly the same thing for him and
imply that, unlike Norman, I have not quite held up my end of
the bargain by becoming an irreplaceable fixture in American
culture.

"Why are you so lackadaisical?!" she demands.

I am cowering with fear and remorse. My mind is scrab-
bling frantically at this word. I don't know what it means. I picture a boy on a hillside. He has no daisies. His eyes are black
holes of stupidity.

"I am embarrassed! I am ashamed that you are willing to be
so mediocre."

I don't know this word either. I am blocked, stammering,
stuck like Emperor Claudius on the first syllable of a reply.

"If you go on in this way, you will become a face in the
crowd. You will go to junior high school and be a face in the
crowd. Do you want to be a face in the crowd?"

I picture heads bobbing in a school hallway. In my mental
picture, the heads begin to lose their shape, wrinkling like apples
on the ground. The features of the faces blur into sameness. All
of them come to resemble, vaguely, the little faces Señor Wences
used to draw on his hand. They are still bobbing, bobbing, spas-
modically.

"Do you remember those men in the Bowery? When you
were in first grade? That is what happens to people who become
faces in the crowd."

Oh, God. Not them. Not those guys again. Help.

I must find out what lackadaisical means, what mediocre is.
I must not be those things. I must not become a Face in the
Crowd. I must not join the incontinent throng of my brothers in
the Bowery.

She is, of course, juggling many complicated feelings. She is angry at me, but her greater wrath is reserved for my father. He is lackadaisical. He is letting himself become mediocre. He is no longer a remarkable boy. Our money is running quite low, and now she is working full time to keep us solvent. Every day, the things that made us all special are slipping, slipping away.

On me, her tirade works, from a somewhat ruthless perspective. I launch myself on a preposterous bends-inducing zoom to the surface. Soon I am near the top of my class. If my zeal flags, there comes, unbidden, the image of me, dirty, ragged, shuffling, unzipping my fly next to a green Pontiac. My zeal reestablishes itself.

❧

As Peter denies Jesus, I deny my father. I deny my third grade self with the toy typewriter.

In seventh grade, I announce to my parents that I intend to become a lawyer. I am going to a private school now, with the children of many lawyers. I can see how they live. In big, chunky, Tudorish houses with mullioned windows. I will forge for myself a career based on certainty and reliability, not a bunch of goddamned elves. I will be the man in the Mustang convertible wearing the double-breasted blazer and the striped tie, not the man sitting in the living room at 1:00 A.M. in his boxer shorts scratching out dialogue on lined yellow pads.

My parents have pieced together some meager earnings and a scholarship to send me to this fancy school. They are hanging on to their cars a few extra years and skipping a few restaurant meals so that I can be a remarkable boy. And what does this get them? A son who cannot hide his own horror at the thought of becoming anything like them. A son who regards them as the Elephant Couple, abject mutants. Let their cup pass from me.

In my defense, I am terrified. At night, I lie in bed and my face burns with the fear of the next day. My status at the school feels so much more provisional than everyone else's. I am on some kind of existential probation and a slip could push me right into the chute that winds through the school building and debouches into the Bowery, on Face-in-the-Crowd Street. And then I think about the way my face is burning. It can't possibly be good for me to have my face burn like that, can it? Probably, I am making myself sick. I will die of Face-Burning Leukemia if I cannot get this under control.

Which thought makes my face burn hotter.

I lose my seventh grade grammar book. I cannot tell the difference between this and the early stages of heroin addiction. Either slip could put me in the Bowery. What will happen? The Council of the Burning Face ponders this all night. I cannot tell my teacher I lost the book. I cannot say "lost." There must be some other word for what I have done. The night turns into a long vocabulary exercise.

"Mr. Friedman?" I say the next day.

"Yes."

"This is Sandy Watson's grammar book from last year. He lives in my neighborhood. He let me borrow it."

"Why?"

"I mislaid mine."

I look at the teacher. A smile is tugging at the corners of his mouth. He knows what a serious boy I am. The care with which I have chosen this word is not lost on him.

"Mislaid?"

"Yes, sir."

"Does that mean you lost it?"

"Yes, sir."

"Fine. Use Sandy's. And try to find yours, okay?"

"Yes, sir."

"And don't use words that way. Use words to say what you mean. Not to hide it. This is English class, right?"

"Yes, sir."

"Then speak English."

❀　　❀　　❀

But I have already discovered lawyerly locution, haven't I?

This lawyer thing is no idle fancy. By ninth grade, I have fallen into the habit of spending vacation days at the courthouse. Put on a tie, catch the bus, head downtown, watch some trials, take notes.

O! What is worse than a geek? A geek with designs.

I don't require Perry Mason drama or James M. Cain heat. I don't need sex-mad lovers and butcher knives. Nope. A run-of-the-bench liability case will suit me fine. I watch a trial in which the plaintiff has injured himself opening a defective soda bottle. The bottle shatters in his grasp, ripping into his flesh. Could the plaintiff have contributed to his own tragedy by opening the bottle in some inventive manner that does not conform to the healthy laws of human understanding? What are those laws? I watch hours of testimony, as if the Scopes trial were unfolding before my eyes. Lawyers get up with church keys and pop bottles. "Would you say it was more like this? Or like this?"

For this Tribunal of Mammon, I have traded in the Court of Pie Powder. I have sold my birthright, my kinship with fairies, for a mess of pottage and broken glass.

I try to persuade myself that this is interesting. I am not a good enough lawyer to win the case. The soda bottle will never be anything but a soda bottle, and the witnesses will never be anybody but who they were. The best of the lawyers I watch have an imaginative flair, but, in the end, they keep their eyes on the ball. I daydream. Would you want a lawyer who keeps a pied à terre in fairyland?

Ah, yes, the fairies. They beckon. They sing in my ear. And then, one day, they bring me a present.

❧

The present is actually a gift from my parents.

In retrospect, it may seem like the crowbar that derails my

Lawyer Train, but that was never on their minds. They don't dislike the lawyer idea. Sure, it's a little crass, but a touch of crass doesn't seem like a bad idea just now. The Romantics have been getting shelled, after all. Maybe it's time somebody was crass.

The present is practical.

It's a blue, manual Smith Corona typewriter. My first.

I'm not going to go into grandiose comparisons, but you know when a thing is right for you. A paintbrush, a baseball bat, a steering wheel, a rolling pin, a piano. The objects of our destiny talk directly to our hands.

That Smith Corona speaks to me. Tack tack tacktack tacktacktack. Ding.

I will use it steadily for eight years. It will go to college with me and clatter under my fingers through long nights of term papers.

But it has one thing to say to me, right away.

"You're not going to be any goddamned lawyer."

Ding.

Five

Straight Outta Roscommon
or
Why History Can Be So Hortful

Sarah Whitman Hooker Pie recommended with this chapter

◆ The Green Bastard

❧

The protagonist of the preflight safety-features film on Aer Lingus is a peculiar, digitally animated man. He has nondescript red-and-blue clothes, short dark hair, a ball-shaped nose, and—this is disturbing—no mouth. Blank space where the oral aperture ought to be.

He does not speak, but even so the safety film seems to mock his mouthlessness. He holds up the tubes on the life vest, tubes into which one blows air. How is he going to do this? The oxygen mask drops down, and the narrator says one must place it over one's nose and mouth. What mouth? Even when we are informed that this is a nonsmoking flight, the safety man is holding a cigarette and lighter.

"He has no mouth!" I say to the screen. "What was that for? To save money?"

Safety Man moves with great deliberation, a kind of robotic t'ai chi, in which motion never speeds or slows, in which the natural herks and jerks of the human body are cooled out. The animators have not solved the basic problem: Natural motion is imperfect.

Safety Man is also oblivious to the Sartrean condition in which he finds himself. Occasionally the frame pulls back to show him sitting amid rows and rows of empty seats. Safety Man is the only passenger on his flight. He doesn't seem worried.

I am traveling to Ireland in April 2001. The flights do, in fact, tend to be uncrowded because Americans know, dimly, that there is (or may be) foot-and-mouth disease in Ireland and that this is either the same as or quite different from mad cow disease and that one or the other can kill you. They picture themselves placed on a pyre of burning carcasses, in a recently purchased Aran wool sweater. They stay home.

I'm going to Ireland, which, I admit, is a pretty hopeless place to look for my father, inasmuch as he never set foot on its soil. Still, as this book swims backward through time, I feel it dragging me back to the place we came from and the time we decided to leave. To Ireland, in 1855, when there were fairies and giants and banshees—in other words, when the contents of my father's mind were real things afoot in the world.

⁓⁂

I stay in the village of Mountnugent, about eighty miles northeast of Dublin. Mountnugent is tiny, not much more than a bridge and a pub and a lake called Lough Sheelin and a few hundred good souls, mostly farmers. The farmland around here is some of the best and richest in Ireland—which has caused people, over the centuries, to do fairly horrible things to one another in order to get it.

I have picked it because of some marriage and baptismal records that show a Thomas McEnroe marrying a Mary Coyle in 1834 and having a series of children. Thomas was my great-great-grandfather. But I am unprepared for the first sight I see as I drive into town. It's a little pub called the Bridge Inn, and etched on the smoked glass of the side door is "McEnroe's."

For some reason I am drawn to a place a few miles away called Ross Castle, a severe sixteenth-century stone phallus encircled by a wall with slots for firing crossbows at one's enemies. The inside has been renovated for guests. I have a room here. I say "here," because I'm sitting in the tower right now, writing this on a laptop. The children of innkeepers Sam and Benita are milling around me, asking questions about the machine. The oldest of the kids, Mark, nine, is reading this over my shoulder.

At bedtime, however, they're back at their farm, and I'm in the castle, in the room at the top of the tower, alone in the green night.

The castle belonged for a time to the notorious "Black Baron" Nugent "whose power could wither and whose word was fate," according to the local histories, and who made the castle "a licensed haunt for perpetrating crimes." The local histories do not come right out and say it, but they manage to imply that the B. B. availed himself of all the perquisites of rank, including having his vassals delivered up to him for sexual depredations. He also seems to have been fond of dispatching them. There was a "Lug an Crochaire" (Hangman's Hollow) near the castle and down the lane is a quarry that, when men began working it, turned out to be full of bones and skulls.

Near the quarry are, supposedly, the graves of Orwin and Sebana. Sebana was a Nugent. Orwin was an O'Reilly. The O'Reillys had a castle across the lough. This gets complicated because of local politics, but the Nugents were Anglo-Normans, the kind of people who got land granted to them by the Crown. The O'Reillys were Celts, more indigenous, with quite a lot of land "beyond the pale," which means outside the enclosed areas that the English types cared about, which is how "beyond the pale" came to mean what it now means—so far out that nobody respectable would care about it.

The O'Reillys would have managed to cut a deal with the Crown. As one of the townspeople tells me: "The local leaders would have wipes and wipes of land, and they'd say to the Crown, 'Look, I'll do whatever you want. I'll fight for you in your wars. But I want to be the boss of my own kingdom.'"

In this way, bosses inside the pale and outside it could coexist, uneasily, for centuries.

The law, for hundreds of years, forbade intermarriage between your Celts and your Anglo-Normans. You can see where this is headed. Orwin, the native-grown Celt, and Sebana, the daughter of the occupying power, fall in love. Legend has it that Orwin tries to get his beloved out of Ross Castle and elope by boat. They drown. It's much better as a ballad. Anyway, the ghosts of one or both of them are thought to haunt the castle, but I am the only guest and not so much as a single rattling chain or mournful sigh do I hear.

There is also—I'm not kidding—"a fairy pass" between the

"hillock and the ringfort." I have to go about twenty miles north to a research center in Cavan to find out there are fairies twenty yards from my front door. Fairy activities are not heavily advertised anymore, especially in the "new Ireland," which is way too techy, too IT-savvy, to have any truck with fairies. Here is a dissonance that is almost Japanese, almost Zen, in its delicacy: Outside the walls that ring the castle are black and white cows. Inside the walls, next to this sixteenth-century hard-on of stone, sitting in the driveway, just as I write this, are two black-and-white faux-cow boxes from a Gateway computer that Sam and Benita have just unpacked. If you threw those boxes over the wall, you might hit a fairy as it moved along the pass. The "trooping fairies" use this particular right-of-way to go to and fro in their "macra shee," their cavalcade, and the whole idea is that if you build your house in their path, the fairies will get mad and beset you with all kinds of misery. At night I go out and stand near the pass. There are shooting stars in the sky and flickerings of borealic light on the distant horizon but nothing you could call a fairy.

The fairies are still there, but the Irish refuse to see them. Safety Man, computer guided and demouthed to silence blarney, is the New Elf, their preferred type of mythological being now.

All of the above shows why it's almost cheating to contemplate and write about your past in Ireland. There's so much goddamned atmosphere per square inch, the ground is heaving with it. All of the above—bone quarry, fairy pass, doomed lovers, hangman's hollow—is crammed into an area of maybe twenty acres. And I haven't even mentioned Miles O'Reilly, "The Slasher," who spent the last night of his life in the castle (apparently when the Nugents and O'Reillys were getting along better) before going down to the bridge at Finnea and doing a lot of slashing, holding off the enemy (Scots, I believe) until he himself died amid the heaped up bodies of his foes. He has his own ballad, too.

Nor have I mentioned Mag Slecht, the "Plain of Adoration," a site in the county where the pagan, pre-Patrick Irish worshiped a foul god, a towering stone idol named Cromm Cruaich. The ancient Cavanians engaged in a form of human sacrifice that makes the Aztecs look like a Bernie Siegel support group.

Here is a bit from a historically accurate poem, author unknown:

He was their god,
The withered Cromm with many mists...

To him without glory
They would kill their piteous, wretched offspring
With much wailing and peril
To pour the blood around Cromm Cruaich.

Milk and corn
They would ask of him speedily
In return for one-third of their healthy issue.
Great was the horror and scare of him.

You think *you* have issues with your parents.

Some of these are not exactly the feel-good stories of the summer, but if you can't get interested in your own past in a place like this, you're just plain not trying.

Where is my past? After a few days here, it sinks in that the McEnroes were probably not players. We were vassals, victims, crossbow fodder. You five guys run across the face of that drumlin and draw their fire. McEnroe, Plunkett, Briody, Moylan, O'Leary. Off with you, then. Good luck, lads, and Godspeed.

The McEnroes were laborers. They didn't own land. They didn't command troops. No one wrote ballads about their heroic, doomed loves. They probably got hanged and raped by the Black Baron; but most of the time they lacked even the epic qualities of victimhood. Most of the time they probably wobbled, like a unicyclist on a wire, between starvation and subsistence.

"They may have had other qualities, good qualities, the kinds of qualities that just don't show up in the histories," I say out loud in the car. I am jouncing down a narrow lane in a rented Nissan, a boxy little thing the size of a large bathtub. To an onlooker I would seem to be alone, but there's a lesser session of the Court of Pie Powder meeting in the front seat. The lanes are often spooky even by daylight. Swirling, brambly vegetation grows right up to the edges and forms walls on both sides, and the roadbed sits low, so that you seem to be running down a chute into fairyland.

"Yes, they may have had skill sets that were not valued," I tell the Court, and its officers chime in helpfully . . .

"You never hear about Miles the Nice."

"John Who Ran Good Meetings."

"Owen the Guy You Could Lean On."

"Hugh Who Planted Peas the Same Way We All Did but Somehow His Were Just to Die For."

This is what you have to face, sometimes. Not everybody can be storied. Not everybody turns up in the trilogy, stabbing a troll with a sword.

Some of us stay home and hoe the bean rows while the big shots battle Sauron.

Sturm und Drang are, after all, the by-products of leisure time. I've been reading *The Lord of the Rings* out loud to Joey in the weeks preceding the trip—this is months before the release of the movie—and I've been getting a little pissed off at the hobbits. It's the first time I've read it in years, and it must have eluded me, in past readings, that Frodo and Merry and Pippin are wealthy idlers. They're all about fifty, and it is clear that none of them has ever had a job. The fact that they live underground and have hairy feet and don't wear shoes should not disguise the fact that they are essentially British nobility. They put in one long hard year of heroics and they're set for life. The McEnroes of the Shire would have had some grinding agricultural job unremarked by Tolkien—notwithstanding his tender enshrinement of the master-servant relationship. Rise up, Sam Gamgee! You have nothing to lose but your trowel!

❧

It's a Friday evening in April. The air is cool and the sun is shedding golden light all over the farms. I pull into the driveway of Father Francis X. O'Reilly, the parish priest in Mountnugent.

He comes to the door of his bungalow. He is dressed in a shirt and slacks and looks to be about fifty, with a spade-shaped face and a thatch of gray hair and eyes that gleam with intelligence.

"I want to apologize for just barging in like this but . . ."

"Looking for your roots, eh?" he demands in an unfriendly voice.

"Um, yes."

"Well go away and look for them somewhere else!" he barks and starts to slam the door.

I step away from the sill and turn toward the Nissan. He catches the door and flippers his hand at me. His face is tightening up with a self-pleased grin.

"No, come in." This has been an act.

"Sit down in there," he says, pointing vaguely to several possible rooms as he goes off to finish a phone call. There is nowhere to sit. The house appears to have been recently burglarized, perhaps several times, with each new ransack occurring before the last one could be set right.

Everything sits in heaps. Books and books and papers and papers and packets of Silk Cut cigarettes and Cadbury chocolate bars and . . . heaps. Heaps that appear to have been heaped on other heaps. Things waiting to be organized into heaps, stuck, as it were, in the pre-heaping stage.

And Father Frank is a gem. He is funny and sad, words that describe eight-tenths of the men in Ireland, but Father Frank has that look of a man who can savor the bittersweet ichor of the nation, let it loll on his tongue.

He digs through the old records written in spidery hand, and we do indeed find the birth notation of my great-grandfather Patrick, in 1841. I tell him more of what I know (courtesy of assiduous genealogical researchers Kevin Curtis and Eileen Germano). Pat was the son of Thomas McEnroe and Mary Coyle, married in 1834. The whole family—Thomas, Mary, and five kids—seems to have emigrated in 1855 and wound up in New Britain, Connecticut, a midsize industrial city with a growing Irish enclave.

"I'm no help to you," Father Frank says wearily.

"Yes, you are."

"No, I'm not."

"Look," I say, "what I need from you is something different from what you're used to being asked for. I already know all this stuff, marriage certificates and baptismal records. I need you to close your eyes, and, based on what you know about this area, tell me who you think they were and what they were doing."

He smiles.

"There's a chance my family evicted yours, you know."

Father Frank is one of those O'Reillys, the slashers and drowners. He spent most of his adult life "away," which in rural Ireland could mean in Istanbul or half-a-county over. The McEnroes down at the pub explained to me that they were not from Mountnugent at all. They were from Virginia. The way they said it you'd have thought they emigrated from Roanoke, but they meant the town of Virginia, Ireland, which is about five miles from where we were standing.

Father Frank's "away" included a stint in Oldcastle, which is about five miles from Mountnugent in a different direction. When he came to Mountnugent, in the churchyard after his first

Sunday Mass, a woman saucily referred to him as a "blow-in" (a newcomer).

"Shut your mouth," her husband growled. "The landlord's back."

I'm interested in landlords, I tell him.

❧

The 1821 census shows a laborer named Henry McEnroe living in the Tonagh townland. A townland is the smallest geographical unit in Ireland. There's no American equivalent. It's as if a neighborhood were drawn with exactitude on official maps.

Tonagh is a name meaning "quagmire," and around Mountnugent it has a special significance. Mention it, and you'll often see a quick flicker of resentment in a person's eyes, because of something that happened in 1847. The average Irish person is not necessarily a scrupulous keeper of his or her own personal genealogy. The past is a world of dirt floors and pigs in the house and chaos and hunger, not an orderly grid of lineage. But the Irish have a keen memory for outrage, and the evictions at Tonagh are discussed as if they happened last week.

The Tonagh landlord turned seven hundred, maybe eight hundred people out of their houses, all in one day. This was accomplished in a pointlessly brutal way, as we shall see—a manner calculated to visit hardship, sickness, and death upon the poor farmers. Even in this country, pockmarked as it is by centuries of small hurt and titanic woe, the Tonagh story has a way of making people suck in their breath.

"I'm wondering if the McEnroes might have been among the families who were evicted at Tonagh," I tell Father Frank.

He looks at me, then looks away. It's about 6:00 P.M., and the low, angling sun is streaking and smearing the land outside his rectory windows. His voice is gentle.

"It's not necessarily true that they were evicted," he says. "The presumption is that they left because of the famine."

He has seen something that I cannot, at this moment, let myself see. That I am greedy for just a little nibble of this tragedy. For my book? For myself? For my sense of the McEnroes as a people who wander under evil stars? Who knows? I'm reconciled to the idea that we did not famously hold any bridges or drown while escaping the family castle. But I'm hungry to find us in the wretched hordes of Tonagh, so ill-treated and direly beset that there is even a local ballad about our misery.

&

There was a family in one of his previous parishes, says Father Frank, who had roots in Mountnugent, and they knew that Frank's family constituted the end of the line of O'Reilly landlords. This family was prosperous, he says, but they were unclear about their own history. One of them asked Father Frank to make inquiries.

Frank mentioned the name of this family to his own father who told him, "They took soup."

During the famine, the Church of Ireland adopted the questionable strategy of offering food to the starving in return for their promise to convert. Soup-takers were expected to be at Protestant services the first Sunday after they accepted the food and to stay there ever after. Wherever possible, they were threatened with eviction if they reneged. Irish stubbornness ensured that this program had very limited success. In a tiny town such as Mountnugent, only two or three families took soup, but one was the family now inquiring of its roots. (Needless to say, they had found their way back to Catholicism.)

"Well, what am I going to do? Taking soup is a mark of shame. This is certainly news they don't want to hear," says Frank.

He let a little time slip by, but the man began to press him. They made a date to discuss what Frank had learned and just as

the dreaded hour arrived, didn't Frank get word that his own
father had fallen and broken his hip, so the appointment was
broken, too, and the whole dodgy business was temporarily
dodged!

More time slid away, and Frank dared to hope that the man
had dropped the matter. The man invited Frank to a dinner at
his lovely new house on a lake. Frank arrived expecting a dinner
party, you know, with various people from the parish attending.

No such thing. Frank arrived to find a full house of dinner
guests, every last one of them—except Frank—from this man's
family. He had invited to this dinner with Frank any person with
two of the clan's chromosomes. The jig was up.

Much food. Much wine. Frank was asked to stand and
deliver the tidings. He had carefully ingested sufficient quanti-
ties of the grape so that the Major Social Abhorrence Centers of
his brain were in a kind of rolling blackout.

He stood. The clank of cutlery, the clink of crystal, the
murmurs and mutters all stopped. He gazed around. "You took
soup," he said finally.

"You know what?" Frank continues the story, "They pulled
through it just fine. It turned out, I think, that they had kind of
suspected something of the sort."

He lets the tale float over the heaps in the room. He lets its
message sink in.

The past is not a good place to go digging for the story that
you want. It's a lane you walk down, unarmored, aware that
almost anything—wolf, hero, fairy, knave—could leap out of the
brush at you.

Father Frank has an evening Mass to give in some other
parish. I climb back in the Nissan, roll down the window.

"Take care, Father," I tell him.

"I hate it when people say 'take care.' It drives me mad.
And it's Frank, by the way." He launches into an explanation of
why he hates this pleasantry, and I don't quite follow it. Because

it's an admonition I guess, but one that's hard to observe. In what sense is he supposed to take care? Is he supposed to watch for pianos that have accidentally been tipped out of overflying airplanes or go a bit more slowly on slippery steps? What made me think he was such a reckless person that he needed encouragement to take care? That's the gist of his problem, it seems.

I find myself drawn into the discussion.

"I had surgery to reattach my quadriceps tendon last year," I began, "and I was gimping around in a leg brace. I noticed that people would take leave of me by saying 'get well.' It seemed a little brisk, a little bossy, you know? Instead of wishing me a gentle recovery, they were kind of telling me to heal myself, right away. 'Get well.' They don't have time for this injury thing. I blame it on computers."

"That's the kind of thing I'm talking about," Frank agrees.

I'm ordinarily horrible at small talk, but for a moment I feel supremely Irish to be sitting in the driveway of a parish priest talking to him about something completely pointless when at least one of us has somewhere pressing to go.

"Well, anyway," I say finally, and then, because I am so involved in thinking about why he hates the expression, say, again, without meaning to, "take care."

"Aaugh!" cries Father Frank, and I throw the car in reverse and speed away before he can kill me.

❧

Boom boom boom boom boom.

I'm up in the tower writing, plickety plick plick, but Sam Walker is worried.

I can hear his broad farmer's feet tromping up the roughly 2,339 stairs to where I am. Boom boom boom boom, here he comes. Sam's wife manages the castle, and from what I can tell, Sam runs a rather large farm nearby. But, a june bug to a Coleman lamp, he is drawn to the guests, and he has gotten wind of my project and appointed himself my Mountnugent Literary Manager.

Today he has decided it is imperative—imperative!—that I go and see Joe Moynagh. He has phoned over to Joe Moynagh and learned that if I leave with alacrity—with alacrity!—I can have an audience with him. Boom boom boom. But if I stay up in the tower plickety plicking on my laptop, this moment will pass, so boom boom boom, he is coming to force me to stop writing and get over to Joe's.

"Okay!" I tell him. Plickety plickety.

It's just that it's so nice to write up here, high up, encased in stone, mournful ghosts swishing and gliding unobtrusively in the background.

Back in the boxy Nissan and down the lane to the main road, past the graves and the quarry and the fairy throughway. And who is Joe Moynagh?

Merely the undisputed expert on the Tonagh evictions, that's all.

This is, I remind you, Ireland in the time of foot-and-mouth disease. I am one of about six American travelers in the country, from what I can tell. There are signs all over the countryside imploring people to dip their feet. Country houses have little basins of water by the doorstep, and the driveways often begin with a spongy mat soaked in some kind of disinfectant. Even Newgrange, a megalithic mound of mysterious purpose in County Meath, with inner chambers older than the Great Pyramids, has been shut down so that we don't spread foot-and-mouth to 5,000-year-old dead kings.

No one has ever seen Ireland act quite this way. Ruthless efficiency! In England, the cows are heaped up in burning piles, and the gods wrinkle their noses at the stench. Ireland has been . . . well, goddamn it, proactive! As a result, foot-and-mouth never really gets going in Ireland.

Information-Technology Ireland has canceled its Saint

Patrick's Day parades, closed down the countryside, and got everybody dipping and wiping like a bunch of Norwegians with obsessive-compulsive disorder. The days of good-natured ineptitude are, it would seem, over. Remember the famine? Well, this time, let someone else have the famine. "We do ones and zeros now," says Ireland.

All of which is why I am standing at the foot of Joe Moynagh's long drive in a bit of a quandary. There are several "No Entry" signs. There's a squishy thing for the car tires to drive across. There's a dipping basin for the feet. There's a sign urging me to join the fight against foot-and-mouth. Am I supposed to (a) go away, (b) drive across the squishy thing, or (c) park by the road, dip my feet, and walk up?

For no reason at all, I pick (c), and when I get up to the house, I say, "I wasn't, um, sure so I, uh, left the car down, um . . ."

Yes, yes, come in, come in. That's fine. Nobody seems to care what I've done. The disease scare is 90 percent over, and people have almost forgotten that there are still ominous signs and contrivances scattered around their properties.

Moynagh has the gentle face of a boy and the saddened look of a very old man. He's middle-aged, with pale blue eyes and a not unhandsome, slightly equine face.

"Going back over history is very dodgy," he tells me. It sounds like a warning. I can leave now and skip the whole thing, if I've no stomach for dodginess.

Not leaving? Well here it is, then.

Joe tilts back in his chair, and the story streams out of him like blood. In 1847, the Irish landlord at Tonagh wanted the land clear to grow grain, wanted to consolidate small holdings into large holdings, wanted to start fresh with a new set of tenants.

So he threw seven hundred people off their land, all in one day.

"It was snowing and sleeting that day," says Joe.

Actually, contemporary accounts report a cold and copious rain, following the autumnal equinox, but the ballad does upgrade it to snow and sleet.

Joe sings a bit of the ballad for me:

All our joys were too good to last,
The landlord came our homes to blast.
In vain we pleaded but mercy no,
He drove us out in the blinding snow.

No one opened for us their door,
For each one vengeance would reach for sure.
My Eileen fainted in my arms and died,
On that snowy night by Lough Sheelin side.

Farewell my country, a long farewell,
My tale of anguish no tongue can tell.
For I'm forced to fly over ocean wide,
From the home I love by Lough Sheelin side.

Every house was "knocked" (dismantled by a bunch of goons wielding crowbars) says Joe, except for one, whose occupants included a man with cholera. The roof of that house was removed, he said, but the walls were left up. Joe believes the house was not razed because the occupants included an agent of the landlord.

"My people were the Briodys," says Joe. "There was an old man in the house who was an invalid. They carried him out and laid him on the ground and knocked the house."

For the record, the contemporary account, by a new priest named Nulty who later became a bishop, is a little different.

I reproduce a chunk of it here, mainly because Bishop Nulty's tone—one of near-hysteria—captures the moment more piquantly than anything I might write.

Seven hundred human beings were driven from their homes in one day and set adrift on the world, to gratify the caprice of one who, before God and man, notably deserved less consideration than the last and least of them. And we remember well that there was not a single shilling of rent due on the estate at the time, except by one man; and the character and acts of that man made it perfectly clear that the agent and himself quite understood each other.

The Crowbar Brigade, employed on the occasion to extinguish the hearths and demolish the homes of honest, industrious men, worked away with a will at their awful calling until evening. At length an incident occurred that varied the monotony of the grim, ghastly ruin which they were spreading all around. They stopped suddenly, and recoiled panic-stricken with terror from two dwellings which they were directed to destroy with the rest. They had just learned that a frightful typhus fever held those houses in its grasp . . . They therefore supplicated the agent to spare these houses a little longer; but the agent was inexorable and insisted that the houses should come down.

. . . He ordered a large winnowing-sheet to be secured over the beds in which the fever victims lay—fortunately they happened to be perfectly delirious at the time—and then directed the houses to be unroofed cautiously and slowly, because, he said, "he very much disliked the bother and discomfort of a coroner's inquest."

I administered the last Sacrament of the Church to four of these fever victims next day; and save the above-mentioned winnowing-sheet, there was not then a roof nearer to me than the canopy of heaven. The horrid scenes I then witnessed I must remember all my lifelong. The wailing of women—the screams, the terror, the consternation of children—the speechless agony of honest, industrious men—wrung tears of grief from all who saw them.

We're right smack in one of those dodgy areas. Joe Moynagh thinks there was one house that was spared, and in that house was a colluder with the landlord and also a case of typhus.

The Nulty account gives us two houses with typhus, each unroofed, and a separate house where there lived a man whose "character and acts" were so despicable that Nulty couldn't keep himself from mentioning them, although he was not comfortable going into any more detail or even naming a name. (That, by the way, strikes me as a supremely Irish trope. Because I am an idiot, because I didn't see this project coming, I brought up the subject of lineage with my father exactly once in our lives, in 1996, almost two years to the day before he died. It prompted a letter from him, not to me but to his cousin Peggy. It had almost a "someone's been around here asking a lot of questions" tone. Going through his papers, I found a draft he didn't send. He writes of their fathers' generation: "All of Pat's boys—except one—were exemplary. Your father had two candy stores and had the gumption to start them." Who was not exemplary? He doesn't say. Does he mean his own father? You see what I mean. Like Bishop Nulty before him, he lifts the pot cover just long enough to let a whiff of perfidy escape and hang in the air. I figured out much later that the exception was Henry, the fifth child of Patrick and Elizabeth. Known as Harry, he ran off to join the circus. He returned to New Britain later in his adult life and was, I gather, a charming man, if not terribly strong in the visible-means-of-support area.)

Why should I care who was the rotten apple of Tonagh?

"It was the Coyle cottage that was spared," says Joe.

Now he looks like a horse who has said something awkward.

You could say I'm as much a Coyle as I am a McEnroe. In fact, that's one of the great jokes of lineage. Let's imagine (falsely) that, when Thomas McEnroe marries in 1834, he is 100 percent McEnroe. His children are only 50 percent McEnroe (and 50 percent Coyle). When his son Patrick marries a Healey, the offspring will be only 25 percent McEnroe and 25 percent Coyle. You could argue that the Healeys, whoever and whatever they are at that genealogical moment, have a bigger claim. They're 50 percent of the identity. And in the next generation, the old Thomas McEnroe stake drops to 12.5 percent and a new family (named O'Connell) buys in, again at 50 percent. You can go back to the old country and find traces of the great-great-grandfather who shares your last name, but he'll have a lot less in common with you, genetically, than your maternal grandmother's sister, whose name you probably don't even know.

Anyway, the Coyle house was never knocked, Joe says. Unroofed but left standing. There was even some talk, he says, that the house was cursed. The local story was that the front door would never shut. There would be plenty of vengeful ghosts, happy to rattle its handle and swing its hinges. The Tonagh evictions were a death sentence for roughly a quarter of the people thrown out.

The reason for this was an unusual instruction from the landlord.

"Everyone for miles around was told not to take them in," Joe says.

There were reprisals threatened against anyone who did.

That left two options. Emigration to America or the workhouse, where families were broken apart and quartered separately, men, women, and children. Diseases raced through the workhouses; floggings were common; you were lucky to survive even a year there.

So by putting out the word that no one was to give shelter to the evictees, the landlord had effectively killed a great number of them. Why do it?

"Nobody knows," says Joe. "There was no rent owed. It was very strange."

Well, there is one explanation. It is possible—although it seems counterintuitive—that owing to complexities in the law of the time, a landlord might have thought he could escape responsibility for his tenants under the "poor law tax" that helped fund famine relief if he not only evicted them, but drove them out of the area.

"Who would have done such a thing?" I ask Joe. "What kind of heartless British bastard would turn seven hundred helpless people out of their homes, knock down the houses, and go out of his way to ensure they had no place else to go?"

"Wasn't the British," he says.

Oh. It was an Irish bastard.

"The landlord Malone and his partners," says Joe. "Their agent was Guinness."

"God bless you for the beer," says Snowbird Toomey, one of my father's characters. "Snowbird Toomey will always be at your service. I am dependably evil. I come from a long line of evil bastards—generation after generation. Breeding counts."

Bob McEnroe, like any good Irishman, could get himself pretty riled up about the British. He once refused to walk into a New York restaurant called The Oliver Cromwell. A couple of Jewish producers were trying to take him there, and my father offered the charming observation that this would be like someone trying to take them to a place called The Adolf Hitler. But I don't think the Tonagh story would have surprised him.

"The landlord was Irish. His agent was Irish. The Irish landlords were no better than the British, and often they were a good deal worse," says Joe, his face contorting with sorrow, with woundedness, and with something unmistakably resembling satisfaction. "In 1854, the land was put up for sale and it was bought by two Irish priests. And they were no better either. This is why goin' back over history can be so hortful."

What is even more hortful is the idea that the Coyles, my kin, may not have behaved honorably.

We took soup, you might say.

"It's too bad you couldn't talk to Kitty McEnroe," says Joe, intruding on my reverie. "She was the last of her generation around here, and she knew some of the old stories."

"Where is she?" I ask.

"She was buried last week. She was eighty-five," he says, adding in a chipper tone, "You just missed her."

⁂

A day or two later, my toaster-sized Nissan rumbles down a country lane to the home of Noeleen McEnroe Plunkett, who is probably my closest relation in Ireland even though—after she gets out her papers and I get out my papers and her husband, what the hell, gets out his papers—we can't really figure out how we're related. Further confusing us is the fact that on two occasions, roughly fifty years apart, someone named Thomas McEnroe has married someone named Mary Coyle.

"When you called, I was sure there was no connection, but now I think there is," says Noeleen. She has lived in Mountnugent every day of her life, and her speech is unusually thick with the local accent, which is vaguely Klingon, lots of noises from the back of the throat.

She is certain that no McEnroes were evicted at Tonagh. It would have been passed along orally, as it has in her husband Oliver's family. He's a Plunkett, one of the other local clans living for almost two centuries alongside the McEnroes, intermarrying liberally. The Plunketts were indeed turned out at Tonagh. They also boast an actual saint, the also-named-Oliver Plunkett who was hanged, drawn, and quartered by the British on trumped up charges involving a completely chimerical Popeish plot to invade Ireland.

Noeleen knows the McEnroes were not turned out of Tonagh because she knows where they were.

"Right there," she says. She points out her window at a crumbly nineteenth-century farm cottage, long abandoned.

"That might be your ancestral home," says Oliver, grinning just a little.

I resist the temptation to dash outside and run my hands

melodramatically down its cool stone walls. Instead I look longer and harder at Noeleen. She doesn't look much like me, but she strongly resembles my father and the rest of his family. She has what is unfondly called "the McEnroe nose," although it might be fairer to say that they have hers. Probably nobody is going to fight very hard for ownership, because it is at once slightly bulbous and hawkish.

I don't know what I expected to find in Ireland.

Well, that's not quite true. I had a vague mental picture of myself on a hill, under a swirling gray sky, falling to my knees and digging my fingers into the earth and announcing myself as "a son of Ballyjamesdough" (or Knockgrafton or some other cool-sounding place). And meaning it. Having some kind of Moment. In this mental picture I seemed to have darker, more tousled hair and stormy, flashing eyes—the guy on the cover of the novels called *Savage Wicked Ravaging Fire of Love,* with elements of Windy from the Association song of the same name.

Instead I found a nose. The McEnroe nose, attached to this nice, somewhat reticent woman.

"Have you noticed in the McEnroes any particular . . . consistent personality trait . . . or any kind of theme running through their lives or . . ." I falter. She is looking at me with incomprehension, and I realize that this is kind of a dopey question—something you might find on your English 223 final exam. What themes unite the protagonists in Arbuthnot's *McEnroe* novels? How do they compare with those suggested by the House of Atreus in Greek tragedy? Give examples that support your points.

On the other hand, I'm flying out of Dublin tomorrow. If there's something here for me to learn, there probably isn't time for me to soak it up in some nuanced way.

"It's just that my father and grandfather had this doomed, anguished quality, and I wondered if . . ."

Noeleen looks out at the cottage for a moment, then looks back at me and says, "No."

And my Irish quest is over. Just like that.

≈❧

Somewhere in the world maybe there's a packet of letters that tell the story of the passage, how Thomas and Mary find the money to get themselves and five children onto a boat and across the Atlantic in 1855.

I can't even picture the trip, but I can at least imagine their new lives in one of the crowded, unsteady-looking houses strewn around what came to be called Dublin Hill in New Britain, Connecticut.

Thomas takes a job in one of the factories. New Britain is already a center for toolmaking. Ten cents an hour, and days that stretch on for ten hours. The children are Margaret, Mary, Thomas, Henry, Patrick. Thomas is born the year before their passage. He doesn't make it to the age of five. The others, including my great-grandfather Patrick, settle in New Britain and live long lives. Patrick takes a job in a mill, marries Elizabeth Healey, another immigrant.

They have seven children. My grandfather Edward is the seventh. The male McEnroes who do not become circus workers go into business for themselves. They own candy stores, ice-cream companies, restaurants, cigar stores, bars, and pool halls.

Edward owns bars. He falls in love with Catherine O'Connell.

≈❧

It is the talent of Catherine O'Connell, over the course of eighty-five years, to make herself invisible.

"Did you ever meet her?" I ask my mother.

"I'm not sure."

"How can you not be sure?"

"I may have met her once."

"This would have been your mother-in-law. Mothers-in-law have a way of sticking out."

"I really don't remember. I think I may have met her just that once."

I try Catherine's niece, Peggy, who remembers all kinds of things, who remembers, for example, certain dresses that her friends wore on dates with my father and the type of car my grandfather drove when Peggy was eight. I ask her questions about my grandmother.

"What was her name?"

"I'm not sure."

"Was it Catherine O'Connell?"

"I don't remember. That sounds like it might be right."

"What was she like?"

"I don't remember much about her."

The name survives on my father's birth certificate. There are no photographs or letters. I haven't the faintest idea of where to look for her grave or even under what name she'd be buried. There is no one left, that I can find, to tell her side of things, if there is a side to tell.

She seems to have lived into the early 1950s, but no one knows where she died or in what year. Or no one is telling.

≈❧

No one is telling anything, except, of course, the scripts.

Sitting on the floor in my own house, I page nervously through *The Exorcism,* the one place where Catherine O'Connell still lives and breathes.

MARTIN BURKE

She's a woman ruled by pride, and pride can ruin
a woman as easily as it can ruin a man. She has
a hunger to be admired. She has . . .

WILLIE BURKE

A thirst for recognition.

MARTIN

A thirst for recognition.

WILLIE

An ache to climb over her fellow men and look down on them.

MARTIN

[*Scowling*]

She's always trying to pass herself off as lace-curtain Irish but her old man was a meterman on a trolley car.

Thus do Martin and Willie, father and son, discuss Bessie, wife and mother. I think the three Burkes are as close as my father dared come to putting his own parents and himself down on paper. The real story was something he could not bear to discuss for most of his life. A few years before he died, I asked him to tell me something, anything about the past. And this is what came out.

Edward McEnroe fell in love with a woman who was lace-curtain Irish. He was shanty Irish. These terms do not come from Ireland. They are, from what I can tell, inventions of the New England Irish diaspora and almost entirely matters of attitude (with a dash of socioeconomics thrown in). The shanty Irish were, well, Irish. They kept some of the old ways, stayed clannish, hid nothing of their roots. The lace-curtain Irish affected Yankee middle-class mores, tried to assimilate.

Eddie owned bars and maybe a pool hall. This was very shanty Irish stuff. Catherine told him there would be no marriage unless he became respectable. Eddie sold what he had and got into the real estate business. My father claimed Eddie learned real estate from a man named Smiley Tatum, which might account for what happened later.

When Robert E. McEnroe was born, my grandmother was distressed. She didn't want a baby. She was an older-than-usual mother for those times. She sent the baby back to the hospital. There was nothing wrong with him. She just didn't want him there. She was tired, overwhelmed, one of the last American neurasthenics.

McEnroe men are named Thomas, Patrick, Richard, William, Edward, Charles, and Henry. Over and over again, like a polypeptide sequence. It makes record-searching a nightmare. Robert is not a McEnroe family name. My father's name is a sore thumb in the McEnroe records. It's more of an inside-the-pale Norman name, the kind that might be worn by someone with unwholesome ties to the king. It is, quite specifically, the first name of the Nugent to whom the Crown granted the right to have a Court of Pie Powder in Mountnugent. My father claimed, unhappily, that he was named after a collie.

After a few days, his mother let the baby come back.

Eddie took his stuck-up wife and his collie son to Miami Beach, where the real estate game could be played at higher stakes. These were the Roaring Twenties, and my grandfather made a bundle, using whatever the Smiley Tatum Method was. By the middle of the decade, he was a millionaire. My father grew up shooting alligators at night. In the summers, Eddie drove his family up to Connecticut in a shiny new Marmon. My father had what was then called a "mammy," a black woman who cared for white children. Inasmuch as his mother did not warm to motherhood, I think it's a fair guess that this African American woman—alas, her name has not survived our pathetic oral tradition—loomed unusually large in his upbringing. In the final year of his life, the home health aides were often black women, and he seemed to find this comforting.

The last complete sentence my father ever wrote was an

unsolicited letter of reference for one of them. I found it, unde-livered, tucked in a book about Dante. The handwriting quivers, and the feel of the note is effortful, as if it might have taken all afternoon to eke out, a great, final heave on the oars of writing to produce this tiny thing. "To whom it may concern: Jean is the best shower girl I have ever had."

But for Bob, the boy, there is damage done in the first twenty-four hours on earth. There is a stain splashed on him—"unwanted," "unwelcome"—like the dye spurting onto the bank robber's loot. Like the loot, he is not fit for use afterward. Or so it feels to him.

Here is my father, in a letter to me, explaining Sylvia Plath: "It is probable that Sylvia's trouble was caused by her relation-ship with her mother . . . This may or may not be true, but what is true is that Sylvia was once a little child who thought that she did not belong in the world."

Fairies steal children at birth. It's in the old legends. Sometimes, in a child's place, they leave a thousand-year-old fairy or a log, which has been enchanted so that it looks to our eyes like a human child. But in some of the stories, the fairies steal a child, bewitch him, and then return him to his parents. And he lives his life with a foot in each world, as a go-between, truly at home in neither place.

Yes, that does sound familiar.

❧

GOD IS OMNISCIENT—Don't try to change his mind.
GOD IS OMNIPOTENT—Don't try to tell him what to do.
GOD IS GOOD—Don't try to blame evil on him.
GOD IS SECURE—He does not require the reassurance of adoration.
GOD IS JUST—Every creature gets either plants or other creatures to eat.

The Nemo Paradox

Now. A few things happen in tight sequence. My father's chronology is, the more I analyze it, probably a little unreliable. But here is his story according to him.

1. My father speaks up in church. His outburst probably resembles that of Henry Nemo, reported above. Of particular interest to my father, who is perhaps thirteen, is the question of why God would require or benefit from any worship, if he is all-powerful and over-stretching. The nuns are displeased. They summon a priest. He is displeased. In my father's version, the boy Robert is branded a dangerous heretic, Thomas More with a cowlick, Abelard with no girlfriend. Too dangerous to roam free, spreading his doctrine.

   My father's version carefully includes him in the romantic procession of Irishmen martyred for their fervent beliefs. In 1916, the year of his birth, the British shot three Irish Catholic poets in a firing squad outside Dublin Castle. One of them was Joseph Mary Plunkett, probably one of Noeleen McEnroe's distant in-laws. It is in this tradition that my dad squarely places himself.

2. In Florida, the penalties for dangerous thinking are slightly less severe. Young Bobby is shipped out to military school. There he breaks rules and is ordered, as punishment, to push some kind of tennis court on wheels. An actual, full-sized, rolling tennis court. Pushing the court from place to place somehow entitles him to play on it, too, and he becomes adept. By all accounts, he was a magnificent tennis player as a young man, another mercurial, left-handed, shot-making McEnroe. And what better Sisyphean torment for a McEnroe and his hubris than to push a tennis court from place to place? God is just.

3. The 1929 stock-market crash comes. Eddie is on the margin, on the bubble, a rickety rope bridge across an abyss of financial risk. The Smiley Tatum Method. Back door not included. He loses everything. He owes even more. He is ruined.

4. Catherine O'Connell McEnroe departs. Abandons the faux-respectable husband and the collie boy. Catches a northbound train. I'd love to write the scene but I haven't a wisp of anybody's recollection to work with. Note on the table? Wailing, demented, operatic episode? The cold strike of a snake?

5. Eddie and Bobby set out in hot pursuit. They catch up with Catherine, somehow, in our nation's capital, but the Flight from Eden continues north to the fatherland, Connecticut. My dad winds up, in some foggy fashion, with his mother and his Aunt Sadie.

In one sense, it almost doesn't matter which details of my father's version are wrong. Each of us constructs a true story of our lives, and it gathers strength as it rolls down the slope with us. My father's story had more force, made more sense to him, explained things better for him than the considerably muddier truth.

In another sense, the errors and omissions are the hard, grinning skeleton holding up the soft tissue of the story-as-told.

Here is my guess about what really happened, based on slim reports from other sources, and my detection of inconsistencies in even the meager set of facts he doled out about himself:

Although the nuns in his church school are probably not overly fond of doubters, I don't buy my father's (ever so Christlike) portrait of himself as dangerous heretic. He is sent to military school, I believe, because he has become a spoiled pain in the neck (a condition confirmed by his cousin) and because his parents want him out of the way while their fortune and their lives are coming unraveled.

And unraveled they do come. Eddie's sorrows run deeper than the loss of his own fortune and the estrangement of his wife. He has persuaded others, friends and acquaintances, to take similar risks, to hyperextend on the sure thing of Florida real estate. His guilt over what happens to them is more than Eddie can bear. (I have no idea how bad things got for the people who followed Eddie McEnroe's counsel, but this was the Crash and the Depression. It is not unrealistic to suppose that Eddie saw irredeemable ruin of whole families, perhaps even a suicide that he believed was his fault.)

Oh, but here. What's this?

"My father was smart at table games. He could beat anybody at cards, etc. When he got out of the loony house we roomed together for a while. I taught him to play chess." Two sheets of that lined yellow paper, covered with whittled black writing, slip out of a folder. My father is dead, and, writing this book, I am spidering around in his files. I have found something. The first draft of a letter to his cousin Peggy.

He is writing about his father.

"Loony house."

"Was my grandfather in a mental institution?" I ask my mother.

Small clearing of the throat. "Yes, that's true. I believe that's true."

"So Dad lived with his mother after they all left Florida?"

"No. I don't think so. He didn't talk about this very much, but I get the feeling she was in hospitals, too."

I'm forty-six. This is all news to me.

"Mental hospitals."

"I think so, yes. I don't know what they called it at the time."

"Let me make sure I'm getting this right. Dad was maybe

thirteen or fourteen. His parents were in his-and-hers insane asylums? For years?"

"I think so."

I feel strangely unmoved by all this, which sounds like something Mr. Spock would say. From a certain standpoint, the news that one's grandfather, grandmother, and father have all been in loony houses is not good. Probably the only thing separating me from them is managed care. I don't feel a whole lot less crazy than they probably did, but these days only Mariah Carey gets to be institutionalized for breakdowns. Anyway, as Willie says in *The Exorcism,* there are worse things than being crazy. "I want to be crazy," he tells his father. "If I'm crazy, it means I'm not possessed. And I don't want to be possessed."

But now I have to construct a third version of Bobby's reality.

Catherine ditches her family, but she takes leave of this world in some other way, too. By the time she gets back to New Britain, she is in no shape to manage her own affairs, much less bring up her son.

Bobby sees it all happening. The mother freezing up, her heart and soul locked deep inside some crystalline structure. The father sinking deeper under the weight of darkness. And one day someone—one of the uncles on Dublin Hill?—sits Bobby down and says, "Boy, you'll be coming to live with us now. Until your parents are better."

The Great Depression settles in. Eddie's other prosperous brothers, the restaurateur and the confectioner, are in the process of losing every cent they have. Grinding misery and woe abound on Dublin Hill. Bobby bounces from family to family, living with whomever will have him. Like a Dickens hero, the spoiled boy is the poorer relation now.

He finds a semi-permanent home east of the Connecticut River—far from the earthy Irish color of Dublin Hill—with his aunt, whose lace-curtain tendencies make Catherine look like a populist. Her name is Sarah Penfield. Mr. Penfield (LeRoy, I have discovered) is not on the premises. Catherine is, some-times, during intervals of sanity. Sarah Penfield—"Aunty"—becomes my father's rock. She will give him succor, stability, sound advice, and something resembling love. She will be Aunt Betsy Trotwood to his David Copperfield on one condition, and this condition, rather than being spelled out, is simply bred into every particle of life with Aunty.

He must reject the McEnroes.

He must repudiate the McEnroes and their Irish ways, their loud laughter and coarse songs, their red faces and flat feet. Their blarney.

It's the old story from Mountnugent. If you want to eat, you've got to renounce.

And so young Bobby takes soup. He takes Aunty's soup and has as little to do with his own kind as he can possibly manage. No McEnroes.

But he begins to construct the foundations of his secret world. He cracks the door and lets in the first few elves. His childhood has been cut abruptly short. He is bitter, betrayed, frightened, rejected. But he has built a trapdoor out of this unforgiving world.

Here is the voice of Willie, the alter ego my father created in his plays:

WILLIE BURKE

Children believe in little people. They believe
in them because they haven't any reason not to
believe in them. It takes time to learn to
doubt. It takes the years of growing up. Each
year that passes means believing in less and
less of the things that dreams are made of and
in more and more of the things that you can
kick and pull and push and tickle, bite, taste,
scratch, and hit with a rubber ball. When you're

all through growing up, you've stopped believing
in a great many things.

                    MCGILLEY
But isn't that natural?

                    WILLIE
All the things you don't believe in are still
there to be believed. They're the charming
things that make childhood enchanting. They're
not less charming or enchanted because children
grow up. They stay the same. Children change.

Let us come back to that draft of a letter to Peggy, slipping
from a folder and fluttering to the floor on yellow-paper wings.
The bit about Eddie and the loony house is, of course, a thun-
derbolt, but almost as startling, in its own way, is the little story
that follows. It is the first inkling I have had that my father ever
saw his father in the tender, amused light that suffused the rest
of his world. It won't seem like much when I share it with you,
but to me, it reads like a wondrous beginning, a squirt of the milk
of human kindness eased out from an udder that had been
blocked for sixty-five years.

He discusses some issues of genealogy, history, and Irish
geography. Then he writes of Eddie's generation, including
Eddie's brother Harry, who ran off to join the circus.

My hat is off to them—all the brothers. Don't forget that it
was a circus worker who knocked up Roe of *Roe v. Wade*.
Since she made history, one can't ignore the rest.
   My father was smart at table games. He could beat anybody at cards, etc. When he got out of the loony house, we
roomed together for a while. I taught him to play chess. We
must have played a thousand games together. I won every
one of them. Based on his earlier experience at games, he
decided I was a chess genius. He went to the Hartford

Chess Club and told them about his son. They invited both of us in for a match. It was bad, Peg, real bad—and then some.

I managed to write this letter so that I worked it up so that I ended talking about me. Let it never be said that the McEnroes lacked egos.

He didn't send it to Peggy. He wrote it late at night, I'm sure, woke up sober, read it again, and decided it was more rapprochement than he really wanted with his long-dead father.

He typed up something more cut-and-dried and mailed it off to his cousin. He died two years later.

He tucked this version, scratched like cave writing on lined yellow paper, in a file and put it away.

For me to find.

❧

"Your grandfather was a darlin' man," says my father's cousin Peggy, "but your father couldn't see that. He had a hard time liking him."

"He could have been a lot nicer to his father," says my mother. "Everybody else loved Eddie."

My father stayed mad at his father until Eddie McEnroe died, two years after my birth. The two men tried to spend time together, but my father's anger was like a hungry animal looking in from the darkness. He had lost too much, and Aunty had carefully nursed in him the idea that McEnroe sloth and squalor had authored all his troubles. Aunty kept him away from the McEnroes for as long as she could, and even when he had grown up, she would tell the McEnroes they were not to distract or embarrass him by making themselves visible at important moments.

"He had a play trying out at Westport, and a group of us decided to go down there for the opening," his cousin Peggy tells me. "We wanted to see Bob after the show and maybe go out with him, meet the cast. Somehow she [Aunty] got wind of this and told me absolutely not. This was an important night for Bob, and we shouldn't bother him or go up to him at all. So we didn't. And later I wondered if maybe it hurt him that his own family wasn't standing around him supporting him."

Is there a pinch of pie powder to be spared for Aunty? She has seen the Irish and their drink and their excesses ruin too many things. Here is a boy, a young man, in whom she sees much promise. He might outlive the curse that seems to hang over his family. But he must be saved. Maybe we can forgive Aunty for being ruthless.

But my father's writing reveals a longing for a lost world of friendship and laughter and music and magic. In script after script, that paradise lost was the bar, the Irish bar. In *Mulligan's Snug,* the bar is where the little people live.

In the plays we meet men like my dad's father Eddie, sweet and foolish and eloquent. Martin Burke of *The Exorcism* is Eddie, and when we meet him in the play, he has dallied in a tavern rather than come home.

SADIE
You managed to find your way to a barroom.

MARTIN BURKE
There were other men there who didn't want to go home. The world is full of men who don't want to go home. The sober men slip quietly into their houses, then tiptoe down to their cellar workshops. They hide in their own basements, these sober men . . . It's sad to think of these men hiding alone in their basements—aimlessly sawing a piece of wood or hammering a nail into something that needs no nail.

The barrooms of my father's plays are, of course, idealized and far more interesting and less sad than real-life gin mills, but in an old newspaper essay he claimed that even his great success, *The Silver Whistle,* and its vagabond hero were inspired by a series of characters he met in an actual Hartford barroom: "While they did not have the same philosophy of living . . . they were just as windy and unprincipled, and used high-flown language in recounting their travels. The old people [in the play] came out of my meeting a little old lady with shoe-button eyes who smelled of magnolias and a trace of gin, and a little old man who was very serious, wore his hat squarely on his head, and with great punctilio presented me with a white mouse."

In his plays, my father uncovered his own yearning for a life he thought was unfairly snatched away from him when his mother forced his father to sell the bars. In *Mulligan's Snug,* the crisis is a plan by Mulligan to sell the bar. The little people think it's a bad idea, and so does the reader.

In his plays, my father told himself what he could not tell his own father: that he wished Eddie had never sold his bars, never left the world of gentleness and laughter for the cruel world of real estate.

⁂

Memorial Day. My mother and my father's cousin Peggy and I are standing in St. Mary's Cemetery in New Britain, the final resting place of many McEnroes.

Clouds swirl in the sky, threatening thunderstorms, offering blasts of sun, pulling the offer off the table. We are unable to communicate, the three of us, without screaming at one another. It's some kind of weird, triangular disease. Peggy is my father's age, which makes her eighty-five today. She is a woman of cheerful features, whose smiling face somehow makes room for the unfortunate Mountnugent nose. Peggy is a legendary talker, as famous for her speech as Miles the Slasher was for his sword. Family members describe her phone calls as though they were alien abductions: "And I looked at the clock . . . and two hours had passed . . . and I had no idea how this could have happened." A doctor, after examining Peggy, looked at her soberly, and said, "You talk too much," as if that were a diagnosis. She stopped going to him.

"Where is my grandfather?" I say. We have been looking at a lot of dead McEnroes. I'm hoping my grandfather's stone may at least make some small mention of my invisible grandmother.

"He's here," says Peggy. "I went to the funeral. I remember my friend Mary Sheehan took the bus. I don't remember what line it was, but there was a bus line . . . It must have gone from Hartford to . . ."

"Peggy!" Already I'm screaming. "The bus is of no consequence. Where have you put my grandfather?"

"I think it was in that section."

"Let's go find the headstone," I say.

"There is no headstone," my mother pipes up.

"No marker?"

"Bob always said he'd handle it."

"My grandfather died in 1956. When did you start to get an inkling that Dad wasn't going to handle it?"

"I told you about this."

"You never."

"I did! You knew there was no marker."

"You lost my grandfather."

"I didn't lose him."

"Well, then, you, somebody, misplaced him. Where is he?"

"The people in the office will know. They have to keep records."

"No one has asked about this man since the day he went in the ground forty-five years ago, and you assume it's on a virus-protected hard drive? I suppose it's pointless to ask where my grandmother is buried."

"We would have no idea."

It's the final bad real estate joke on Eddie McEnroe, played by the son who never forgave him anywhere but in the pages of his writing. Eddie's last lot was never developed.

Real estate, my father observed, is not for the tender of heart.

Here is part of a letter he wrote to a younger friend, a man my father suspected of having tender-heartedness. The younger man is thinking of doing some investing in real estate:

> I don't want to sound like an evil bastard, but one doesn't buy from fat cats . . . one buys from someone who is hurting—a man who wants out—a man who has holes in his soles.
>
> In order to make money, one must buy at the right price. This means torturing the aged, and grinding widows with small children. A seller must have real motivation to sell or one can't drive the price down . . . Lots of money has been made inesting in real estate—lots of money has been lost.
>
> Sincerely, Bob
>
> p.s. The missing letter in the last line is "v."
> p.p.s. One doesn't use the children to grind the widows.

The letter is written ten years before his own death and thirty years after his own father died. Has he figured out yet what he's really saying? Eddie McEnroe—the man who failed him and deprived him and his mother of a livable life—was too gentle, too tender, for real estate. He could not have evicted the widows and children of Tonagh or taken advantage of the man with holes in his soles. Eddie so deeply blamed himself for the misfortunes of people who took his advice that it broke his nerves and put him in the asylum. Snarled and glowered at by himself and his son for decades, Eddie is innocent of letting the world and his family down.

In *The Nemo Paradox,* Henry Nemo awakens from a fugue state. His frontal lobe has been sliced like Thuringer. He has no way of knowing whether he committed the murder of which he stands accused. He announces to his diary that he is going to study the case, break out of the mental hospital, and go on a quest, if that's what it takes.

"If I get the idea that Henry Nemo did it, Henry Nemo's going to pay," writes Henry Nemo. "If I come up with a reasonable doubt, Henry Nemo is not going to pay—no matter what."

It's such a McEnroe idea—that forgiveness and blame lie out there somewhere, beyond the gates and walls and bars of ourselves, sealed in a Thermos and buried in the sand of a beach at the end of a long road.

Everything we need is inside us. It took me a trip to Ireland and back to figure this out. And most days, I've forgotten it by 10:00 A.M. You heal from the inside out. Everything we need is inside us. I should write it on the bathroom mirror.

And Bob McEnroe? Did he figure it out?

I keep coming back to that musty script of *The Exorcism,* which seems so obviously an allegory for his family. He writes it before his suicide attempt. He writes it during the latter part of my childhood, when the trips to the zoo and the days in the sunshine were trailing off a little. When you grow up, it suddenly occurs to you that the guy tossing the ball to you when you were eight, the guy who lay on the floor putting together the erector set with you, the guy who helped you with the "new math," whatever that was—that guy spent his other hours wrestling with mortality, sexuality, the snakebites of the past, and the poisons of the present. Maybe playing with you was the only break he got all day, some days, the only moment when he didn't feel as though he were going mad. But he was also keeping secrets, sparing you the details of adult manhood. And the way you know all this, when you finally grow up, is that you catch yourself doing it, too: playing "pig" or messing with the Nintendo football game or reviewing the facts of the French and Indian Wars and hoping the whole time that your kid can't hear the shrieks and lamentations echoing inside you.

I'm on the floor, still, reading *The Exorcism*, hoping for an explanation, a more complete account of Bob McEnroe's childhood. I see he has drawn Martin, a character resembling his own father, Eddie, with obvious affection and maybe a twinge of condescension.

Bessie, the character symbolizing Catherine, is cold, judgmental, controlling, pitiless. She is the last person we see on stage. When I come to the end, a sickening chill sweeps across me.

After a botched attempt to lead an exorcism, Bessie is revealed as an apparent fraud with no real supernatural powers. The other players, rushing off on errands of love or folly, leave her sitting alone in semi-darkness. The play concludes:

[*BESSIE takes out a cigarette. As SHE raises it*
to her lips, a flame appears before her. SHE
lights cigarette.]
[*CURTAIN*]

That's how far he got, rethinking Mommy. Either the devil herself or the devil's apprentice.

Six

In Which the Court Adjourns

The last Sarah Whitman Hooker Pie
- ◆ Rip Van Winkle's 20-year-old stale, moldy, dusty, rusty Humble Pie, with a tiny keg of potion to wash it down

꩜

There comes a time when Aunty can't hold him anymore. Bob makes his way out to the University of Chicago but then runs out of either money or patience. He will have, as an adult, not one single story or remembrance to share about the University of Chicago, which makes me think it is another hard time.

But while there he sees the movie *Winterset*. It's an epiphany.

"That is what made me realize what I wanted to do. I wanted to write things kind of like that," he says later.

Winterset stars Burgess Meredith. It was released in 1936, when my father was twenty. It's based on a Maxwell Anderson play, which is based loosely on the Sacco and Vanzetti case.

The play is about, not incidentally, a young man's quest to vindicate his father.

Bob comes back to Hartford and goes to work for United Aircraft. He learns about the engines of airplanes. He likes it there. Parts fit together and make a whole. There hasn't been a lot of that in his life.

He lives in a boarding house in an area known as Asylum Hill. He gets back together with the McEnroes. Aunty is still consulted on all major matters, but he and his cousin Peggy grow close, almost like brother and sister.

"He wasn't like the rest of us," she says. "He had already decided he was going to be somebody different, somebody important. He was going to write plays."

When the war looms, he tries to enlist, but the army doesn't take him. He never tells anyone why. His demons and dragons are out on his surface in those days, and it seems possible he is judged psychologically unfit.

There are lots of young women around, and he is very handsome.

"The girls loved Bobby," says Peggy. "I mean, they really loved him. I had a friend who bought a new dress any time he asked her out on a date. But I think he only fell in love once."

She is a pretty brunette, an ex-bobby-soxer who once tailed Sinatra around Hartford and got into a snowball fight with him. She and her roommate give great parties. He is at some of them, and they catch each other's eye.

When they marry, Aunty does not attend and refuses to speak to her, ever.

❧

"There was a time when they would go and visit her, at whatever facility she was in at the time," my mother says.

"What? Who would go visit whom?"

"Bob and his father. Would go visit Bob's mother."

"Really? This is something they kept doing all those years?"

"I think it's more like something they started then. This was in the early 1950s."

"How did it go?"

"I don't know. They would never say anything when they got back. I don't remember how many times they did it. It was something they tried, I think."

I can see them now in their long coats, in their hats, smooth, taupe felt with black bands.

It's a day in November, with the lightest of rains falling as they stand outside the house on Chestnut Hill in Glastonbury. They've made their visit. A little small talk in a dayroom and then all three dropping into silence as they watch the rain bead up on a window.

Now it's over. The men have driven back, and they stand outside Bob's house, Eddie wondering if he should just get in his car, Bob wondering if he should ask Eddie in. The rain lets up into mist and mixes with wood smoke as the two men stand, afraid of catching each other's eye.

Leave them there. Or leave them in the dayroom, all three of them, each stranded on a different rock, separated by stormy seas. But for a moment, the waves quell and the winds gentle, enough so that they can look across the waters and see one another. "I'm here." "You're there."

⧉

I'm back to scouring his dreaded appointment books, hoping to reassemble him in the air in front of me.

In 1995, I find myself sitting on a line.

"I have the impression that Colin does not like me," he has written.

My heart crumples like a paper lantern in a drill press. Even at that late date, do we still not get it? Just three years to go in his life, and we haven't figured out anything. I have loved him, strained against him, worried about him, worried even more about me. Have I forgotten to do what most people do with Robert E. McEnroe? Enjoy him. Watch his slow, strange dance with the fairies and relish his peculiar reports from that world.

"I have the impression that Colin does not like me."

⚛

My friend the writer Anne Batterson was once staying in Sligo in the home of a Mrs. Rafferty.

"Do you believe in fairies?" Anne asked her.

"No, but they're there," said Mrs. R.

She had sealed up the fireplaces because fairies like to sneak into your house that way.

It does no good, of course.

The fairies get in anyway, everywhere.

MULLIGAN
Willie, are they there? Can you see them?

WILLIE BURKE
[*Looking slowly around the room*]
Why, they're everywhere.

MULLIGAN
[*Smiling*]
Are they now.

WILLIE
They're on the tables, on the backs of chairs, on picture frames—everywhere you could think of.

DOUGHERTY
[*Skeptical, mocking*]
And how tall are they?

WILLIE

[*Measuring with thumb and forefinger*]
No bigger than that.

GALLAGHER

[*Also mocking*]
And they wear little coats and pants and little
shoes with silver buckles.

WILLIE

[*Nodding*]
Some have brown coats and orange britches; some
wear blue and red; some have green and yellow—all
different colors. They make the room glow with
color. You can't imagine how beautiful it is.

GALLAGHER

And they wear little colored hats and caps?

WILLIE

[*Nodding*]
They whirl and whistle and sing. Sometimes they
all whirl at once. Then all the colors dance in
the air. It's the loveliest thing you ever saw.

Those are Bob McEnroe's words, not mine. It's lovely to see those fairies, but they're not here to help us.

That's why, even after we bury him, my father has to die one more time.

He has to die in me.

For the private, evening drinker, the era of recycling provides a kind of upbraiding. Once a week, you grab the handles of a sturdy blue bin and haul a week's worth of brain and liver damage down the curb. The wine bottles all look familiar. You stopped and got that one on the way home from work on Tuesday night because you knew it would go so well with the marinara sauce, and

you bought those two at the wine tasting Saturday and that one . . .
Lying on their sides, jumbled up with the olive oil bottles and
roasted pepper jars they seem . . . numerous.

In the late spring of 2002, I put down the bottle. I was never
a drunk, just a damaged soul who drew alcohol around him like a
soft blanket as each day darkened. And I liked the taste of the
stuff. Maybe that's what my father told himself, too.

I miss it, but I miss it like an old friend who died, not like a
lover whose arms I can't stay out of. We heal from the inside out.
Fairies, alcohol, love, sex, Jesus . . . you sort of have to shut them
out for a while and let the world inside you knit itself together. As
I write this, I'm still in that altered state that comes when you stop
drinking. The recovery people call this the time of "kindling,"
because you crackle with a bright, watchful, sudden brightness.
I'm kindling these days, feeding a bigger fire that burns bits of my
father and his fairies away. They're flying skyward and out of my
life, like sparks in an updraft.

So my father dies one more time.

☙

Shortly before my book is finished, the McEnroes tell me I
must seek out my father's cousin Billy. In his prime, Billy was the
most enchanting of the McEnroes. Bill was the guy in the liquor
business, and he looked all his life like some kind of harvesting site
for the Irish phenotype. He had style and the smile and the wise-
cracks and the suits and the whimsy and the cigars. He was
Central Casting's Irish-American liquor salesman, circa 1958. He
was my father, without fairies. Without demons, too.

Go and see him, they say. He's not particularly well-grounded
in the present anymore, but he remembers the past quite vividly.

Pie powder is streaming in ribbons across the sky as I pull
into the parking lot of the place where he lives. "Assisted living" is
what they call it. Some kind of counterpoint to "assisted suicide,"

I guess. It's an attractive, slightly formal place, and I find Billy sitting in the sunroom. Chairs, backed up to the wall, form a ring around the perimeter of the room, and every single one of them has a nicely dressed old person in it. It looks as if some kind of afternoon tea dance were taking place but no one had quite mustered the resolve to ask another person out onto the floor.

Billy is happy to see me and knows exactly who I am.

But his clarity has been slightly oversold. Like most old people, he has been culling side players and supporting actors from his memory, so that when he "remembers the past" quite lucidly, what he remembers are the details of his own life.

"You remember my father, Bob McEnroe."

"Oh, yes."

"Do you remember him as a boy?"

"Not really."

"Do you remember whether, during the Depression, he came to live with your family? I had heard that, when his mother and father went into the hospitals, he came and lived at your house for a while."

A slight shake of the head.

"I don't remember that."

"Do you remember anything about my grandmother? Did you ever see her? She was Catherine O'Connell. Eddie's wife."

"I don't remember her."

"Tell me about New Britain. Tell me about Dublin Hill."

Ah, well, Billy can remember plenty. He even remembers the address of his childhood, 27 Harrison Street. And his father's restaurant down on Commercial Street. It was right near a fire station and a police station, which was helpful, because those fellows liked to eat.

I press a little more for details about my father, the departure of Eddie's family to Florida, anything.

A helpful look crosses his face.

"You know who you ought to talk to? You know who would know all about that?"

"Who?" I am rendered a little breathless. Maybe I'm about to hear the name of the Virgil who can lead me through my underworld.

"Talk to a fellow named Bob McEnroe."

A pause.

"You mean my father?"

Billy seems untroubled. "No. Bob McEnroe. Fellow about my age. Maybe a little younger."

"Playwright?"

"That's the guy."

He touches my knee.

"And if he gives you any trouble, you tell him I said it was okay to talk to you."

This is starting to feel familiar. I resist the urge to ask him who wrote *David Copperfield.*

I steer us back to the Depression and we talk about his own experiences, the ruin of his own father, their flight from New Britain.

"He lost everything. And then he still owed. He went down to Florida, too, for a while, my father, but that turned out to be the worst thing he could do, because his money was in all the wrong places when the crash came."

"I'll bet you my grandfather Eddie was the one who talked him into it."

Poor Eddie. Wouldn't it just be the case that he pulled his older brother down with him?

"It was a sad time, wasn't it?" I say.

"It was a very sad time for the McEnroes. One fellow jumped out of a building."

"Who was that?"

He ponders for a moment and then, "Bob McEnroe."

"Bob McEnroe jumped out of a building?"

Billy smiles, as if a sudden hilarity has struck him.

"Yeah! He was okay, though. He walked away from it." He smiles even wider, as if the whole thing has gotten funnier. His square sodblock face lights up. "He dove, you see. That's it. He dove out the window."

I'm smiling, too. Almost laughing. This is some kind of great joke, but neither of us is quite sure how it goes.

&

We're coming to the end here. Possibly you have located your hat already and are shuffling your feet below your seat, to see if you've left anything there.

I feel the need to remind you about pie powder. It's unwise to talk to fairies and pointless to drink yourself right up to the edge of their woods every night. That doesn't mean life is without magic, even redemptive magic, but most of it is stored within you. Forgive yourself. Forgive others. Drop the charges. The Court of Pie Powder is a place where that can happen.

Close your eyes.

Not while you're reading this book, mind you, but in a separate, quiet moment.

Close your eyes.

&

He had the impression I did not like him.

Dear Bob,
I love you
If you read this.

Pie powder is drifting down, settling softly across the Tonagh lands, quieting Lough Sheelin, filling in the wounds and the cracks in the crust of life. Like the year's first snow soothing the ravages of November, pie powder is coating the scars of history.

Pie powder twinkles like pixie dust in the twilight, and I see people emerge from the tree line of time to hold out their palms or catch it on their tongues, like fairy communion. There are the Coyles of Tonagh, who took soup and kept their house. Forgive them, forgive them. And Norman Cristina, who set fires and saved my father's life. See how the pie powder sprinkles onto their cheeks as they look up. There are Joey and Thona and the woman with the baby on the street in El Paso. There is my mother, twirling slowly, arms outstretched in the warm blizzard. And who is that older man with the ruddy cheeks and the smiling eyes? Eddie? Is that you? Have you come out to let the pie powder waft down and collect in those soft gray eyebrows? Far off toward the horizon, through the haze of white, I see the dull, dark shape of another woman moving slowly through the powder, her hand held up to touch her chin. Catherine. Grandmother. I could follow her tracks in the white dust, but she would only recede from me.

Forgiveness and healing. Pie powder can fix everything. Can't it?

Pie powder is drifting down. I am having a vision.

In the middle of a meadow sits a judge's bench. A man walks toward it through the swirling, scattering storm of flour. He is a figure from one of my father's dreams. His gray hair falls to his shoulders from a middle part. His beard is full and arrow shaped. He wears a linen suit and high black boots. He carries bagpipes under his arm, for theatrical effect. He climbs up, sits down, and bids me approach. He stares at me for a long while.

"It's millennia of flaw and failing that bind the human race together as much as anything else," he says, finally.

"What does that mean?"

"It means you can't duck soup. That's a joke. But it's true: We're all soup-takers at our worst and weakest moments. You weren't a perfect son. So? He was an easy person to hurt because he walked around with all those tipsy little cups of poison balanced inside him. One little jostle and he was down for the count. He built rooms and rooms of illusion because he couldn't stand to live in the real world. You'll never find him in those rooms now. You can't heal him, and you can't slay him. He's gone, and it's time for you to let up on yourself a little bit."

"Yes."

"Do you know what Gödel's 'incompleteness theorem' says?"

"Not really."

"It says that within any system of mathematics, there will always be some propositions that cannot be proved either true or false using the rules of that system." His manner softens. "I'm dismissing all charges against you. You're free to go."

Pie powder is drifting down across field and farm and in the park where they've taken Joey to feed the ducks.

Down by the pond, I can see my mother and my son, talking and laughing. Grandmother and little boy, helping each other. We're all doing assisted living.

Closer to me, standing off to the side, through the haze, I see a man, ruddy faced, a little stooped, with hair as white as a polar bear's.

That's the guy I should talk to. Bob McEnroe. He knows the whole story.

But he has never told it, and now he is gone, and he was awfully good, it turns out, at covering his tracks. Like a master spy, he had a network of drop-boxes and false addresses so vast and complicated that he was able to slip out behind it. He made up a universe of fairies and giants and ghosts, among whom he could live more comfortably.

Pie powder is falling down. The inscrutable man with the polar-bear hair is breaking off pieces of bread and tossing them forward into the warm air of a spring morning. His eyes are crinkling, and his mouth is drawn in a tight half-smile. He will never tell the whole story. He is looking far away and very close and nowhere. He tosses more bread in the air, and it's gone.

It may be a trick of the landscape, but I don't see any ducks.

Epilogue

He was doing long division, one of those onerous tasks made even worse by its name.

"Long division." All of the punishing monotony is right there, implied in the words. It's like root canal. They should call it something else.

I remember long division as a dark night of the soul in my own childhood. Something about the dwindling, narrowing quality of the computation made it especially depressing. Subtract, pull down another digit, subtract, until you are left with . . . nothing. Long division is a series of partings. My father helped me with my math. I help Joey with his.

"Every parting gives a foretaste of death; every coming together again a foretaste of the resurrection," said Schopenhauer, who was forced to do excessive amounts of long division in the late eighteenth century and concluded that man's natural state is a constant striving without satisfaction.

When Joey's long division was done, he looked out the window and saw the snow, fine as sugar and driven by a night wind.

"Let's go out. Let's take the dogs somewhere," he said.

It was 9:15. A school night. Why not?

We drove to a fairly secluded school. There was one lonely van in the parking lot, the day's snow heaping up on its top.

"Who would be here?" he demanded.

"A hardworking teacher?"

"Must be nuts. I would leave the minute I could."

In the snow, his spirit swelled and puffed, like a sail catching wind. I envied him. He is twelve. I am forty-seven. Lately, life has been looking very sick and sad to me. Subtract, subtract, subtract. Long division. The best I could do, it seemed to me, on this night, was to hand the baton of enthusiasm off to him, let him marvel at the world, maybe pretend to join in.

"Look at this!" He pointed to an enormous maple, its hundred arms crooked out, striped with muscles of new snow. Behind the maple, the winter sky was red. "Why doesn't somebody paint a picture of this?"

In my mind was the title of Ram Dass's book, culled from the advice he got—when his name was still Richard Alpert—from an ex-surfer going by the name Baghwan Das. "Don't think about the past. Be here now. Don't think about the future. Be here now."

So there I was, watching the finely grained snow drift through the halos of parking lot lights, bearing my sorrowful secret—that life winds down and we die. And there he was, oblivious, exuberant, being here now.

As we pulled out of the lot, his expansiveness had spilled over onto the van and the person working late.

"We *need* hardworking teachers, right?" he demanded. "It might be a custodian, too. Kids don't appreciate custodians enough."

He reminisced. At his old elementary school, there had been a special day on which the custodians were honored in the cafeteria, and once, on Veterans Day, one of them, Rocco, had worn his army uniform. Middle school seemed a little brisker, busier, maybe too busy for this kind of observance. Was there

...denly worried, that Rocco had been called up
... former fifth grade teacher, a marine, is in
...o' is a great name, isn't it?" he chattered.
...ing about the snow, he acknowledged, that
...ive and happy. The year's first snow is not a
...der. It is real. You can rub it between your
...too. The only son of an only son of an only
...our line.

Back home, he put on his pajamas inside out, because stud-
ies in the Berne supercollider indicate that wearing one's pajamas inside out can cause school to be canceled. It has something
to do with the behavior of quantum particles.

He was still sort of a Diamond Jim Brady of goodwill, light-
ing his cigars with five-dollar bills of agape.

"Where is Mrs. Farrow now?" he wanted to know, peering
out his bedroom window. Her house, across the street, had been
sold. She's in assisted living.

"I should go and visit her. You should set that up."

He was quiet for a while.

"I miss Charlie," he said. This is Mrs. Farrow's husband,
who died some time ago. He had out, on his bed, an old book
Charlie had given him. It's called *I Remember Distinctly*.

"I miss Bob." This is his grandfather. "I miss all the people
who have died."

None of this was said piteously, but matter-of-factly, as if he
had glimpsed his place in the cavalcade, the tribe of gypsies living and dead, rumbling through the dark, and singing across the
marches of time and space.

Precious little of this enlightenment would survive the
night, not when the pajamas and the snow failed to do their jobs,
not when school opened without even—o, perfidious dawn!—a
ninety-minute delay.

But for a while, in the hours before bed, in the year's first
snow, he saw what my father could never see and what I long to

see—the connections, the abundance, the joining of things.

The resurrection.

multiplica